Praise for *Meditation: The*

"The spirit of meditation is con[...] [...] this book. Mr. Glover's clear instructions will enable you to meditate, and his enthusiasm will inspire you to meditate. If you read this book, you'll be filled with the spirit and will meditate—gratefully!"

> Henry Reed, Ph.D.
> *Your Mind: Unlocking Your Hidden Powers*
> *The Intuitive Heart*

" . . . the essence of the use of meditation as Harry Glover sees it can be summed up in his words, 'We begin to love ourselves as we are loved. We begin to see ourselves as God sees us. We realize we are no greater but, also, no lesser than any other soul in the earth, regardless of their rank, position, or wealth. This realization is worth its weight in gold and transforms us into the person we have always wanted to be.'

"In my experience, this is truly what can happen as we consistently use meditation in our lives."

> Gladys Taylor McGarey, M.D., M.D.(H),
> Scottsdale Holistic Medical Group, P.A.,
> Scottsdale, AZ

"Harry is a walking encyclopedia of information on the Edgar Cayce readings and other philosophical topics."

> Randy Fultz, Ph.D.
> Holistic Health Practitioner
> Dallas, Texas

"Nothing is a more powerful teacher than the sharing of personal stories and practical examples, especially when they are supported by solid philosophy and well-reasoned research, as the reader will find in this book. Harry

Glover's explanation of the Cayce approach to meditation comes alive from his clearly presented evidence that these methods really do work. They will bring you peace of mind, reliable insights for making decisions, and greater health. It is valuable reading for the newcomer to meditation and to the experienced meditator who's ready to be reinspired."

Mark Thurston, Ph.D.
Professor of Transpersonal Psychology
Atlantic University
The Inner Power of Silence: A Universal Approach to Meditation

Meditation:

The Light
from
Within

Meditation:

The Light from Within

Edgar Cayce's
Approach
to Life's
Challenges

Harry Glover

ASSOCIATION FOR
RESEARCH AND
ENLIGHTENMENT

A.R.E. Press • Virginia Beach • Virginia

A.R.E. Press
215 67th Street
Virginia Beach, VA 23451-2061

Glover, Harry, 1927-.
    Meditation: the light from within : Edgar Cayce's approach
to life's challenges / by Harry Glover.
        p.   cm.
    ISBN 0-87604-429-1
    1. Meditation. 2. Cayce, Edgar, 1877-1945. I. Title
BL627.G57   2000
291.4'35—dc21

                                    00-062072

Cover design by Lightbourne

Dedication

On the spiritual level, this book is dedicated to the Christ within, which has guided me all of my days in the earth, long before I became consciously aware of His presence, and who is the true author of this book.

On the human level, this book is dedicated to my three children, Kristine Elaine Morse, Keith Evan Glover, and Kevin Thornton Glover, all of whom I am most proud.

Contents

Acknowledgments

My heartfelt thanks and gratitude to the following persons, without whom this book would not have been possible:

To Joyce Impola, who constantly and lovingly encouraged me to record my thoughts and experiences in a book that could be shared with others on the subject of meditation. Her seven years of arm twisting finally got through to this slow-moving Taurean. Spirit and Shar's gentle pushing provided the necessary discipline and desire to get it done.

Many kudos go to my soul buddy and friend, Velda Hoenig, who graciously and unselfishly agreed to edit my work. I rarely, if ever, disagreed with her editing. Her input kept the book simple, easy to read, and, I hope, very understandable. She, too, lovingly and gently encouraged me to write this book. Her caring support gave me the final impetus I needed to start and complete the project. I am deeply indebted to her.

To my good friend, Shelby Morgan, who provided me with her personal computer, simplifying and speeding up the work exponentially. To her friend and mine, Pat Wolla, whose computer expertise was my salvation as I wrestled with learning all the ramifications of the Microsoft windows software, which I had to learn from scratch. To Cameron Halkett for his time and effort given in aiding me to complete the required computer data.

To Charles Thomas Cayce, who was kind enough to write the foreword for this book. I am most grateful to him for taking the time out of his very busy schedule to read and comment on my labor of love.

To Mark Thurston, Gladys McGarey, Henry Reed and others who read my manuscript and gave me their feedback.

Foreword

*E*dgar Cayce's readings suggest that we "share what we have found helpful" in life, and, thus, help make the world a better place. Harry has done this in his book on meditation. In addition to a clear description of "how to," his personal stories make the purpose for meditation come alive. Meditation is both the wind in his sails and his anchor in rough waters.

This is no guru preaching from on high. Harry is right in there with the rest of us dealing with job loss, divorce, death, severely disturbed children, and financial problems. I found his book both hopeful and helpful.

Charles Thomas Cayce, Ph.D.
President, Edgar Cayce Foundation

Introduction

*E*very man and woman on this planet has a story to tell. No matter how unimportant or insignificant we may consider our lives to be, in the sight of our Father-Mother God, no life is unimportant or insignificant. Each person has had experiences and events occur that would be inspiring for another to hear and to share. This is the reason I wrote this book. If only one other person receives guidance and inspiration from my experience, then the time and loving energy given to writing this account will have been valuable and worthwhile.

This book is about meditation and how the daily practice of meditation can enhance anyone's life physically, mentally, and, above all, spiritually. It is also somewhat autobiographical; many of my personal experiences in the practice of meditation are included. And there are many references to Edgar Cayce's 14,000-plus psychic "readings," given in an unconscious state over a period of forty-three years, from 1901 through 1944. For any not familiar with this outstanding person and his work, I highly recommend three books: *The Story of Edgar Cayce: There Is A River*, by Thomas Sugrue; *Edgar Cayce: The Sleeping Prophet*, by Jess Stearn; and *My Life as a Seer: The Lost Memoirs of Edgar Cayce*, compiled and edited by A. Robert Smith. All three are available through the A.R.E. Press. You may order these books by calling 1-800-723-1112.

You may contact the organization founded by Edgar Cayce and his associates, the Association for Research and Enlightenment (A.R.E.) at 215 67th Street, Virginia Beach, Va. 23451 or at 1-800-333-4499. They will give you any other requested information about the A.R.E., an open-membership and nonprofit research and educational organization formed around, but not limited to, the work of Edgar Cayce.

THE EDGAR CAYCE READINGS

Let me comment on the veracity of the Edgar Cayce readings, since much of my information regarding meditation is derived from them.

Edgar Cayce, 1877-1945, was the most extensively documented and possibly the most accurate psychic in history. In an altered state, he gave "readings" in response to questions put to him. Most of the readings were about the questioner's physical health, but eventually, the readings touched on an estimated 10,000 topics, including reincarnation, meditation, spiritual development, psychic ability, and astrology.

The readings are generally estimated to have an accuracy of between 85 and 92 percent. There are some who believe that, if Cayce said it in his readings, it must be true. I do not share that opinion. He made mistakes in his readings, as outlined in the book, *The Outer Limits of Edgar Cayce's Power*, by his two sons, Hugh Lynn Cayce and Edgar Evans Cayce. There were times when his physical, mental, or emotional condition was not up to par, and his own readings said that, at such times, his information could be inaccurate or faulty. I base the credence I give the readings on the usual accuracy demonstrated in his physical readings, given for those who had illnesses of various natures.

The readings urge us to take the information and test it in our own lives to discover for ourselves how accurate or inaccurate it is. Those persons who accepted and applied Cayce's suggestions for their afflictions were either completely cured or immeasurably helped. Meanwhile, those who chose not to follow his instructions obviously received little or no help. Because the 9,603 physical readings he gave over a period of many years were quite effective, I have the faith and the feeling that his spiritual direction and information are also reliable.

I embrace the readings' admonition to not let them become a religion, cult, ism, or schism. Cayce also urged us not to let his information interfere with our own religions. Instead, we should let it be a study practiced in addition to our church education, and let his readings help us to become better fathers, mothers, sisters, brothers, sons, daughters, husbands, wives, and friends.

This book contains no thesis. I did not write to please the scholars or the literary critics. I wrote this book for the common man. I have purposely kept the language simple and free of erudite words. I once had a college English professor use the word *hyperpolysyllabic-*

sesquipedalianism (the excessive use of big words) on me in class. I vowed then to always keep it simple in my lectures and my writings.

The purpose of this book is to share what I have learned from the daily practice of meditation and to encourage readers to take up the discipline. Meditation is the closest thing to being a true panacea for one's problems in life that I have ever found in my more than thirty years of religious, parapsychological, and metaphysical study and research or as close as one can find in this three-dimensional earth. All the reader needs is the discipline to sit down every single day, seven days a week, and make the effort to meditate.

I will discuss what meditation is; how to prepare for it each day; what to expect in the experience of the silence; what physical, mental, and spiritual enhancements you can expect in your everyday life; how it will help solve almost any problem with which you may be confronted (by which I mean that the guidance and strength obtained through meditation will permit you to accept and deal with whatever problem or challenge confronts you), and, most importantly, how it will teach you truly to love yourself, thus aiding you in learning to accept and love others.

I do not claim meditation is an easy discipline to perform every day. For most of us, patience is required to become fully aware of meditation's advantages and power. However, since new cosmic energies seem to be flowing into the earth and the "vibrations" appear to be rising in the last few years, that may no longer be true. I feel new adherents to the practice of meditation may well experience a more rapid awareness of its results in their lives.

Meditation by individuals brings Light into the world, *Light*, here, being synonymous with Love, God, Truth, Energy, and Universal Law, and it is sorely needed in the earth at this time. There are fifty or more little wars being fought all over the planet, and a great deal of cruelty and lack of Love is being expressed by much of humankind. Meditators become Light transmitters, bringing Light into the earth to dispel the darkness expressed here. As I have said many times in lectures and seminars, if only one person becomes a new daily meditator and brings more Light into the earth, then the seminar or lecture has been successful. The earth, and all its souls manifesting themselves in human form, are in critical need of this Light. Most especially we need to know we are carrying this Light within ourselves and can manifest it by our personal choice and action.

So let us explore together the amazing wonders, marvels, and Light-giving powers of the art and science of meditation. I invite your questions and stories of your personal experiences. Address all inquiries to: Harry Glover, c/o the A.R.E. Press, 215 67th Street, Virginia Beach, VA 23451. Please include your return address, area code and telephone number, and a stamped, self-addressed, number 10 (business-size) envelope.

A Note on *A Search for God*

Frequently, I quote material compiled by the fifteen members of the original study group, that met with Edgar Cayce for eleven years. This group received an enormous amount of spiritual information from the readings in the 262 series, which was later published as *A Search For God, Books I and II.* These books form the foundation for the study groups the A.R.E. sponsors all over the world.

A Note on the Reading Numbers

The Edgar Cayce readings are organized with a numerical system in which each person requesting a reading was assigned an individual number. Thus, in reading 1422-3, 1422 is the number for that questioner, and 3 means the third reading for that person.

A Special Note on Levi's
The Aquarian Gospel of Jesus the Christ

This classic metaphysical book has been a major influence on my life and meditation, and I will be drawing from it extensively. (Readers already familiar with this book may want to pass on to Chapter 1.) The book was first published in 1907, and is available now in a restored and fully reedited version from DeVorss Publications. The author, Levi H. Dowling (Levi), was an ordained minister and held two medical degrees. He was told in meditation that if he meditated between the hours of 2:00 a.m. and 6:00 a.m., he would be given the ability to read and decipher the akashic records on the life of Jesus. (One reason I highly recommend this book is that it covers the *entire* life of Jesus, including the missing years from the ages of 12 to 30.) Levi was instructed to put that information in a book for all to read in the Aquarian Age.

The word *akasha* comes from the Sanskrit, and the akashic records contain the record every soul leaves upon the skein of time and space. This includes every thought, emotion, feeling, and action experienced by each soul from its inception. It is referred to in the Bible as "the book of God's remembrance." (Does it not behoove us, then, to keep our thoughts and actions as loving and positive as possible, to enhance our soul growth?)

I should add here that most scholars would not consider *The Aquarian Gospel of Jesus the Christ* to be an authority on the life of Jesus. The Cayce readings tell us, however, that the soul recognizes spiritual truth, regardless of its source. This book, to me, represents an interpretation of the truth. Cayce was once asked:

> (Q) We are told that *The Aquarian Gospel of Jesus [the] Christ* is taken directly from the akashic records. Is it historically true, and should I use the facts in my book?
>
> (A) It is the experience of an individual, or of Levi, who was in that experience and wrote from his own experience. To him it was an actual fact. 2067-2

Regarding the term *Aquarian Age*, let me offer an explanation to those who may not be familiar with the phrase.

On that one day at the beginning of spring (the equinox) when day and night are exactly equal in length, the sun rises at a certain point on the horizon, and there will be a constellation behind that point. If that constellation is Pisces, say, then we may speak of that year as being in the Piscean Age. However, there is a small wobble in earth's axis, as there is with a top or a gyroscope, which causes this spring equinox point to appear to move very slowly backwards against the constellations, at the rate of one astrological sign every 2,160 years. The equinox point has moved approximately one whole sign since just before the time of Christ, when it began to rise in Pisces instead of in Aries. The equinox point is, therefore, now very close to the boundary between Pisces and Aquarius.

The Cayce readings state that we entered the Aquarian Age in the year 1936 (1602-3). There is some disagreement among students of astrology and metaphysics regarding this date; some believe the age started in the latter part of the nineteenth century and others believe we have not reached that point as yet and that it will be in the early part of the twenty-first century. The reason there is disagreement over whether we are now in the

Aquarian Age or still in the Piscean is that, unlike the signs, which are exactly thirty degrees of arc, the constellations vary in size, some larger and some smaller than thirty degrees of arc. I go along with the 1936 date, since Cayce's readings have proven to be accurate in the area of physical healings and very consistent in the information and dating given in the past life readings.

The Aquarian Age represents the expansion of man's consciousness and freedom of expression. It is not difficult to see how this has taken place since 1936, as we have focused increasingly on greater tolerance, freedom, and equal treatment for all types of people and all sorts of beliefs and lifestyles. Hence, *The Aquarian Gospel of Jesus the Christ* is, in my opinion, a book for all people, races, and religious beliefs.

1

Why Meditate?

Why should you meditate? To begin with, it is vitally important to understand the spiritual nature of man. That man is a spiritual being, first and foremost, is a basic truth promulgated by the Edgar Cayce readings, the Rosicrucians, the Theosophists, and even by Jesus himself, according to the gospels in the New Testament. We as souls (spiritual beings) project into the earth and into physical bodies via the birth process. We are not bodies with souls; we are souls who come into the earth in three-dimensional human form, using this form to navigate this three-dimensional world of ours. If Cayce

1

was right, there never was a time when humanity did not exist (*humanity* here being used in lieu of *soul* or *spiritual being*). Humanity has always existed, because we are literally part and parcel of what we call God. Again, according to the Cayce readings, each soul is an expression of God and has that spark of the Divine within it. Jesus said "the kingdom of God is within you" (Luke 17:21) and "Is it not written in your law, I said, Ye are Gods ?" (John 10:34). If we can understand that we are spiritual beings and are a part of what we call God, that we have always existed as entities before our birth into bodies, that we exist as entities (souls) while in the flesh, that we will continue to exist as entities in Spirit after the physical bodies die, then we will have a clear foundation for understanding what meditation is and what meditation can do for us. When we meditate, we contact the God part of ourselves, become one with Him in Spirit and consciousness, then bring forth more and more of the attributes of His Love and Energy into our physical and mental expression.

The great teacher Jesus said it all very concisely when he instructed us in the two great commandments: "Thou shalt love the Lord, thy God with all thy heart, and with all thy soul, and with all thy mind. This is the first and great commandment. And the second *is* like unto it, Thou shalt love thy neighbour as thyself. On these two commandments hang all the law and the prophets." (Matthew 22:37-40)

Ah, but living and applying these two commandments in our lives are no easy accomplishments for most of us. Here is where the daily practice of meditation is especially valuable. This is not to imply that meditation is the only approach in learning to apply these two great commandments, but I can say unequivocally that meditation is an effective and capable discipline toward that end.

One's own personal experience and exposure to any

theory or practice is the best crucible, and I can attest to the effectiveness of meditation energy in my own life in reaching these two goals. As I move closer to the ability to love myself as God loves me, thereby finding it much easier to love others, I discover I also have an enhanced ability to live cooperatively with the two great commandments given by Jesus, which, in turn, allows me to keep the Ten Commandments given in the Old Testament.

Let us now turn to the question of whether God is impersonal or personal, as this question often arises as we begin to make contact with Him in meditation. We read in the Bible that God is no respecter of persons, which I interpret as the impersonal nature of God, in that God does not play favorites but treats us all the same by loving us all impersonally and equally. Now, how do we get the Father to become our personal God? There is a story that is a beautiful analogy and that provides an answer:

A man had an aviary with well over one hundred birds in it. Each day, he entered the aviary to feed and water his birds. He loved all of his birds equally and showed no favoritism towards any of them. One day, during his caretaking duties, a little finch flew down and perched on his right shoulder, chirping and talking to his master in a loving, friendly, and very personal manner. The man observed the finch's action and chirping and began talking back to him, telling him how pretty he was and how much he loved him. At that point, the man became a personal master to the bird rather than an impersonal one. In a like manner, God becomes a personal God to us when we make the move to become personal with Him. The Christ spirit sits, quietly and patiently waiting, within the bosom of us all, ready to respond the moment we call upon Him. I imagine His response might be, "I thought you would never ask."

I can say from experience, once you have sincerely

and actively included God in your life by your personal choice, be prepared, for your life will take on new direction, and you will never again become bored. In fact, you may feel you have opened Pandora's Box, for all kinds of opportunities for soul growth and service to mankind will be presented to you. You may even experience some pain as your "karma" gets speeded up. However, the fact you are now making the effort to meditate and contact the God within you will bring you all the loving support and direction you need to solve whatever problems may arise.

It may, at times, be hard to accept, but our pain can become our joy. As Kahlil Gibran said in his beautiful rendition of *The Prophet,* in the chapter on Joy and Sorrow:

> . . . Your joy is your sorrow unmasked. And the selfsame well from which your laughter rises was oftentimes filled with your tears. And how else can it be? The deeper that sorrow carves into your being, the more joy you can contain. Is not the cup that holds your wine the very cup that was burned in the potter's oven? . . . Some of you say, "Joy is greater than sorrow," and others say, "Nay, sorrow is the greater." But I say unto you, they are inseparable. Together they come, and when one sits alone with you at your board, remember that the other is asleep upon your bed . . .

2

Free Will and the Energies of Meditation

Our greatest gift from God is free will—the ability and freedom to choose what we think, what we say, how we express ourselves, and how we react to life and the situations life brings to us.

The will is an attribute of the soul. If we choose a high spiritual ideal, the daily practice of meditation actually strengthens the will and greatly assists us in making positive choices. I often tell my meditation seminar participants that they have to make only one important choice—use the will to choose to meditate every single day, which, in turn, will improve all their other choices or use of their individual wills.

A story in the Cayce readings can help us grasp the meaning of creation itself and the creation of souls with free will. Consider the following summary of what the readings say regarding the soul's creation:

God desired companionship. He, by His desire and Mind, expressed Himself into illions and illions (my word for very, very many) of sparks of energy of Himself and His Nature. He gave each soul an identity and a soul name, along with His gift of free will, and charged us all to love each other, to love Him, and to create wonderful expressions of His Love and Light throughout the universe.

He gave us free will because He wanted us to choose to love Him and to follow His lead in loving and creating. He could have created us as robots or automatons, but then we would not be truly voluntary companions. Would you like to have a spouse or child who is an automaton? Yes, you might program the other person to love you in all ways and at all times, but would that be real companionship? Would you not rather your spouse, parents, and children *choose* to love you, even though it might break your heart for them *not* to love you? Do you not feel wonderful when such persons in your life *do* choose to love you?

God not only gave us free will. He also gave us free access to Energy. To me, good and evil are only states of the *use* of God's Energy, and evil simply means the *misuse* of that Energy. If man uses electricity for lighting, heating, powering his tools and conveyances, such is a positive use of energy. Should he use electricity for killing, destroying (such as the electric chair), weaponry, this is a negative use of that same energy. Energy is energy and does not care how it is used. It is impersonal. *We* control the use of God's Energy by our choices. When we use it positively, we love, and create the good things for ourselves and our brothers and sisters. We teach our children the laws of Love. We choose to be of service to others. When we use it negatively, we destroy, indulge ourselves selfishly, murder, rape, pillage, rob, and are cruel, unkind, and unloving.

It is important to understand all of this because, as soon as we begin to meditate, our choices about how we use Energy will start to be greatly amplified, as will the outcomes of those choices.

When we meditate, Energy rises through the seven chakras or psychic centers, and the released Energy is automatically directed to and manifested through our spiritual ideal, whatever that ideal may be. If the ideal is positive and loving, we become a more positive and loving person; if it is negative and selfish, we become just that, a more negative and selfish person.

We each choose our own spiritual ideal. It may be God, the Christ, Jesus, the Buddha, Mohammed, Confucius, Love, Harmony, etc. It is our choice. But be aware that we can have a negative ideal if we choose. Cayce said we can become a good crook if that's what we want to be. The Energy we raise is impersonal, and we can use it in any way we choose. Of course, one must be aware that using God's Energy in a selfish, self-indulgent manner will create some negative karma for oneself.

There are seven major chakras or energy vortexes in the human body, and these are visible to people who see etheric Energy. The chakras follow the same order as the spectrum of visible light, beginning with red and ending with violet at the forehead.

Cayce associated these chakras with specific endocrine glands, as follows, and pointed out that the *true* order for energy rising is not to the crown but *over* the crown to the *forehead*, following the shape of the shepherd's staff:

Gland	Location of gland	Site of Chakra
7 pituitary	see Figure 1	forehead
6 pineal	see Figure 1	crown
5 thyroid	throat	throat
4 thymus	behind sternum	heart
3 adrenals	on kidneys	solar plexus
2 leydig	gonads+adrenals	below navel
1 gonads	genitals	perineum

Let me now quote from *A Search for God, Book I, Meditation*, "III. Preparation for Meditation":

When we quiet the physical body through turning the mind toward the highest ideal, there are aroused actual physical vibrations, as a result of spiritual influence becoming active on the sensitive vibratory centers in the body, stimulating the points of contact between the soul and its physical shell. Let's trace this activity.

When we attune ourselves to the Infinite, the glands of reproduction may be compared to a motor which raises the spiritual power in the body. This spiritual power enters through the center of the cells of Leydig glands (located in the genitive system). This center is like a sealed or open door, according to the use to which it has been put through spiritual activities. With the arousing of the image, or ideal, this life force rises along what is known as the Appian Way or the silver cord, to the pineal center in the brain, whence it may be disseminated to those centers that give activity to the whole of the mental and physical being. It rises then to the hidden eye in the center of the brain system (pituitary body), which is just back of the middle of the forehead. Thus on entering meditation there arises a

Figure 1: The Endocrine Glands

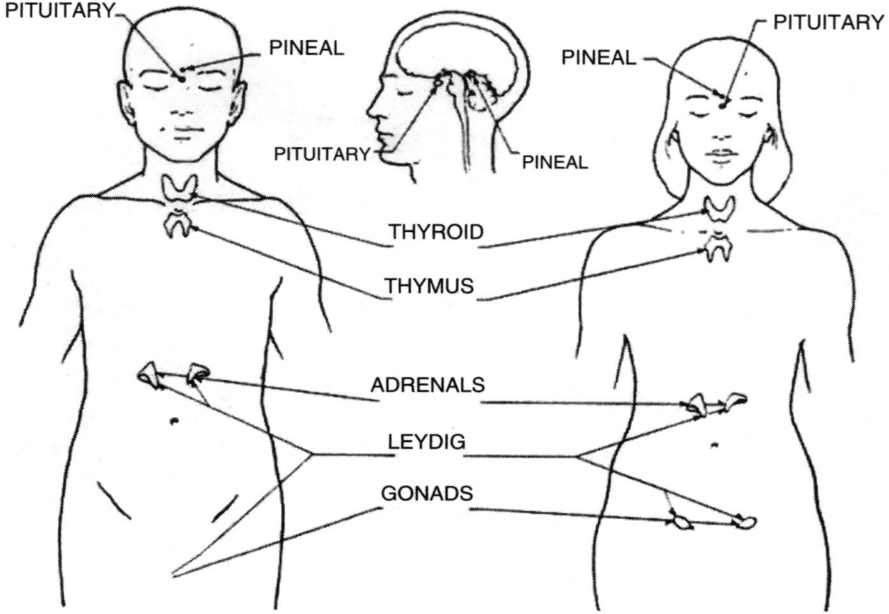

definite impulse from the glands of reproduction that passes through the pineal to the pituitary gland. Whatever the ideal of an individual is, it is propelled upward and finds expression in the activity of the imaginative forces. If this ideal is material, there is built more and more into the body a love for, and a tendency towards, things of the earth. If this ideal or image is of a spiritual nature there is spiritual development. Psychic forces are only an awakening of soul faculties through activities in these centers. If an anatomical or pathological study should be made for a period of seven years (which is the cycle of change in all body elements), of an individual who is acted upon through the pituitary gland alone, it would be discovered that such a person trained in spiritual laws would become a light to the world. One trained in purely material things would become a Frankenstein [monster] without a concept of any influence other than material or mental.

This material clearly outlines how the energy can be misdirected if a positive ideal is not embraced, and that is why we will turn now to the ideal itself.

3

What Is Your Ideal?

What Is an Ideal?

By far the most important step we can take in preparing for meditation is to set our spiritual ideal. An ideal is a model, a standard of perfection or excellence, a peak or pinnacle we wish to achieve or to move towards. *The New World Dictionary of American English, Third College Edition*, gives the following for the word *ideal*:

> 1 a conception of something in its most excellent or perfect form 2 a person or thing regarded as fulfilling this conception; perfect model 3 something

that exists only in the mind 4 a goal or principle, esp. one of a noble character

Without a spiritual ideal, we are like a ship without a rudder, being tossed to and fro by the wind and the waves. In the physical realm of daily living, this is like being pushed and pulled in whatever direction outside, earthly influences take us, rather than in a direction we choose.

Remember, though, we are spiritual beings and need to recognize ourselves as such. Although we all have the God spark within us, He will not interfere with our choices, as we have free will. It is therefore up to us to assume responsibility for our lives and turn within to establish a spiritual ideal. This is important because, by choosing our spiritual ideal, we are choosing the direction we wish to go with our spiritual growth, thereby acknowledging our spiritual heritage.

The following Cayce reading excerpt succinctly clarifies and sums up the importance of one's spiritual ideal:

First, as indicated, *find self.* Find what is self's ideal. And as to how high that ideal is. Does it consist of or pertain to materiality, or spirituality? Does it bespeak of self-development or selfless development for the glory of the ideal? And be sure that the ideal is rather of the spiritual. And this may become, as given, the first psychic experience of self's own inner soul, or self's own guide—as may be chosen. And do not be satisfied with a guide other than from the Throne of Grace itself! . . . And who better may be such a guide than the Creator *of* the universe? For He has given that "if ye will seek me ye may find me" and "I will not leave thee comfortless," but if ye are righteous in purpose, in intent in desire, "I will bring *all things* to thine remembrance" that are needs be for thy soul, thine mind, thine body, development. 440-8

An excellent source of material for additional insight into the subject of establishing a spiritual ideal is found in *A Search For God, Book I*, Lesson 3, entitled, "What Is My Ideal?" The following excerpts come from this chapter:

Our ideals are ever present; they are either consciously or unconsciously the basis for the motivating forces in our lives . . .

From the physical, mental, and spiritual viewpoints our ideals are patterns by which we endeavor to shape our lives. We must understand the meaning of "The Oneness" and merge our physical and mental ideals with the spiritual ideal of the soul. Our spiritual pattern should not be trimmed to fit us, but we should grow to fit the pattern, whose Maker and Finisher is God . . .

The true ideal is the highest spiritual attainment to be reached on this material plane . . .

. . . The ideal cannot be made by mortals, but must be of the spiritual nature that has its foundation in Truth, in God. Know the first principle:

The gift of God to man is an individual soul, which may be one with Him, and that may know itself to be one with Him and yet individual in itself, with the attributes of the Whole, yet not the Whole." 262-11

Such must be the concept, or the ideal, whether of the imaginative, the mental, the physical, or the spiritual body. All may attain to such an ideal, yet never *become* the Ideal, but be one *with* the Ideal.

With this ideal once set, there will be no fear. There

will come to each of us that grace to dare to be a Daniel, to dare to stand alone. We attain our ideal by seeing the Father in others.

Henry Reed, Ph.D., noted psychologist, author, and researcher, wrote an excellent paper entitled, "A Lesson In Setting Ideals," adapted from his book, *Your Mind*,[1] from which the following is taken:

> An ideal is something for the individual who formulates it. It is something the individual *does* believe in, not something an individual thinks everyone *should* believe in. On the other hand, one way to see if the ideal you've chosen is really what you want is to ask yourself what kind of world would it be if everyone followed that ideal? Would it be a kind of world you would want to live in? . . .
>
> One definition of an ideal might be a person's highest value . . .
>
> An ideal is a valued pattern of perfection that is used as a standard of excellence, quality, or spirituality. Ideals having to do with spiritual values cannot be defined exactly. An ideal is contained in the spirit of the law, not its letter. The "Spirit of '76" was the expression of an ideal for the founding of America. The Declaration of Independence and the Constitution were attempts to put that spirit into writing. These documents are imperfect attempts to define the ideals of a nation. America itself is an imperfect expression of its own ideal, yet the spirit of the ideal is there, alive and functioning as a guide . . .
>
> Evaluating a mousetrap for its safety is evaluating it according to an *ideal*, not according to the

---

[1]*Your Mind: Unlocking Your Hidden Powers*, published by A.R.E. Press. An earlier edition of this book was published by Warner Books as *Edgar Cayce on Mysteries of the Mind*.

idea of a mousetrap. We can think about an ideal mousetrap, but it means going beyond simply the mousetrap idea. It means thinking about some absolute standard of perfection, in terms of ideals like safety, humaneness, or efficiency, that would be used to distinguish a better mousetrap from an ordinary one. Yet a mousetrap can still be a mousetrap without being even close to an ideal one.

Because an ideal can never be satisfied, it acts as a perpetual motivator. An idea can be a motivator, but since it can be satisfied, it doesn't motivate for long...

Ideas and ideals both create the reality of a life, but only ideals will create a life that is satisfying. The true measure of a person is the ideal the person steers by...

Defining an ideal is the first step in an adventure into higher consciousness . . . Developing an ideal life begins with the definition of an ideal.

The Nature of the Christ

Before discussing the ideal, let me define my understanding of the term *Christ*. The word *Christ*, to me, is synonymous with the word *Love*. It is a conclusion derived from a number of metaphysical/philosophical sources, one of which I wish to share with you now. This extract comes from the Introduction to *The Aquarian Gospel of Jesus the Christ*:

What is meant by "the Christ" as the word is used in this book?

The word *Christ* is derived from the Greek word *Kristos* and means *anointed*. It is identical with the Hebrew word *Messiah*. The word *Christ*, per se, does not refer to any particular person; every anointed person is christed. When the definite article "the" is placed before the word *christ*, a definite personality is indicated, and this personality is none other than a member of the Trinity, the Son who had a glory with the Father-Mother before the worlds were formed.

According to the teachings of all ancient masters, this Son is Love; so the Christ is Love, and Love is God, since God is Love.

I think the Apostle John was trying to convey this idea when he said, at the beginning of his gospel, "All things were made by Him; and without Him was not any thing made that was made." (John 1:3) We are all of one substance. As the Cayce readings remind us, we all have the spark of the Divine within us. We can call that one substance God or Logos or Christ or Love.

Let me further clarify my view of this idea. Let's look at the Father-Mother God principle as an expression of positive and negative energy, or two sides of one energy, the positive side as thrusting and pushing forth, the negative side as receptive and nurturing. Now the Father-God Energy impregnates the Mother-God Energy, and of that action is born the Son of God or the Christ as pure Love. So, to me, the words *Christ* and *Love* are synonymous.

I have a different view of the name *Jesus Christ* from that of the average Christian in America. I do not see the name *Christ* as Jesus's surname. Rather, I see the term *Christ* as an office, position, or state of consciousness to which Jesus was elevated. I see Him as *Jesus who became the Christ.* So we, too, can become elevated to a state of Christ Consciousness and learn to love as He did. I do not mean to imply that Jesus was not the son of God— He was most certainly. However, so are *we* sons and daughters of God who have not yet reached that perfected state He very ably demonstrated. Did He not instruct us that we can do greater things than He did? We are all Christs in the making. Each day, as we meditate and make contact with the Christ or God within us, we become more and more like Him, here a little, there a little, line upon line, precept by precept, thereby inching closer and closer to the perfected state we pursue and desire.

Meditation will not get you to this state overnight. Meditation will assist you in getting there by teaching you to let the God-force flow through you. As you allow this energy to express more freely through you, both in prayer and in your everyday interactions with others, you become a channel or instrument through which He can give His Love to all of His children. In this way, day by day, we become more and more Christ-like, just as Jesus did.

Choosing an Ideal For Yourself

When I was first introduced to the Cayce readings and began meditating, I did not have the benefit or knowledge of the significance of a spiritual ideal. I looked up the word in the dictionary and began to experiment with first one spiritual ideal and then another. I formed an ideal from various words, such as peace, harmony, truth, service to others, kindness, gentleness, etc. After much experimenting, I was able to settle on my own ideal, as it became apparent to me that all of these attributes were encompassed in the word *Christ*. *The Aquarian Gospel*, as just quoted, indicates that the term *Christ* represents the pure Love of God. Therefore, to me, this was the ideal I should adopt as my personal spiritual ideal. In my mind, I could not have a higher ideal than the Christ, but this ideal may not be suitable for everyone. A person of orthodox Jewish persuasion may not accept the word *Christ* due to its association with the man Jesus. But each faith seems to have associated with it a person or other being who best exemplifies the ideals of that religion. It is not important which particular manifestation, embodiment, or form of an ideal we choose. What is important is that we feel our choice to be the highest we can relate to at the time.

And now I would like to give you, the reader, the opportunity to do this for yourself, if you haven't already done so.

In my meditation workshops, I conduct a short reverie, followed by writing our physical, mental, and spiritual ideals in three concentric circles. Please refer to Figure 2, on page 22. The reverie is designed to assist those just beginning to establish a spiritual ideal for themselves. I give it here, in detail, to assist anyone who would like to set (or reset) an ideal.

I suggest you record the following reverie on an audiotape, being sure to allow the various time delays. Then, as you play the tape back to yourself, you can actually participate in the reverie without having to stop and read the information. Here is the reverie:

Get comfortable in a chair of your choosing and begin to relax with slow, deep breathing. Breathe as deeply as possible, filling the lungs to their capacity, breathing through the diaphragm to get the lower lobes of the lungs full of air. Breathe in very slowly, counting to ten or twelve, holding the breath for one or two more, and then continuing with the count, while slowly exhaling, until you reach somewhere between twenty and twenty-four. (The numbers here are not important; what *is* important is to find a count that works for *you*: not so hard as to be stressful, but slow enough to be relaxing.) This, properly done, should permit about three full breaths per minute. Do this deep breathing for about three minutes or so, to get as relaxed as possible.

This reverie is designed to assist you in choosing a spiritual ideal. For the next few minutes, follow these instructions as given. I will be asking you to consider an ideal mentally for thirty seconds and then asking you to *feel* that ideal for an additional half minute.

Continue to breathe deeply and slowly. Let your body relax. Let your mind relax. Imagine yourself sitting outdoors on a beautiful day, alone under a tree. It's very peaceful and quiet. You feel a deep sense of wanting to understand your purpose as a spiritual being, wanting to grow and to learn. Consider these qualities which might be a part of your spiritual ideal.

The first one is *peace*. What does peace mean to you? Use your analytical mind to think about a definition for that word. (thirty-second pause) And now, begin to feel a sense of peace. Move beyond thinking about peace to actually *being* peace. **(thirty-second pause)**

The next quality is *harmony*. What does harmony mean? Just rationally think about harmony for a moment. (thirty second pause) Then begin to feel a sense of harmony—harmony within yourself. Feel harmony with other people you know—family, friends, co-workers, and with all of life. **(thirty-second pause.)**

The next quality is *brotherly love*. What does that mean to you? What would be a definition of brotherly love? (thirty-second pause) Now begin to experience that awareness, that desire within yourself to love others. **(thirty-second pause)**

Now, *understanding*. What does it mean to be

understanding? (thirty-second pause) Next, how does it *feel* to be understanding? What is the deeper, inner meaning of the word *understanding*? **(thirty-second pause)**

Faith. What is faith? (thirty-second pause) How does it feel to have faith? What is it like to experience faith? **(thirty-second pause)**

Eternal. What is a definition for *eternal*? (thirty-second pause) Something within us *is* eternal. Try to feel that part of yourself, be aware of that part of yourself. **(thirty-second pause)**

And finally, *service*. What does it mean to be of service to others? How can you be of service to others? (thirty-second pause) Now, see if you feel the desire within yourself to be of service. **(thirty-second pause)**

Then, keeping your eyes closed, take one minute and think about other qualities which, for you, would be a part of the highest spirit you want to guide your life. (One-minute pause) Now take those qualities, along with peace, harmony, brotherly love, understanding, faith, eternalness, and service and bring them into a oneness of consciousness. Bring all of those qualities together into your heart. Rest, be still, and be aware of that state of consciousness. **(thirty-second pause)**

Now, let a word or a phrase come to your mind that, for you, will represent that unified feeling or state within yourself. (thirty-second pause.) When you have the word or phrase, open your eyes. Using a pencil, write that word or phrase in the center circle of your chart. This is your spiritual ideal for now. You may want to change it later. **(end of exercise)**

This is simply an exercise to aid anyone in need of selecting a spiritual ideal. Once you establish your spiritual ideal, you can then set about selecting your mental and physical ideals, which you can enter in the middle and outer circles, respectively. You might choose more than one mental and physical ideal, of course. Just be sure the ones with which you choose to work are related to the chosen *spiritual* ideal. It is the spiritual ideal that will be the basis for manifesting your mental and physical ideals. As said earlier, the spiritual ideal governs the mental/physical ideals, and, thus, is the most important. Also, it is the *spiritual* ideal we are seeking to allow to manifest in the world. The mental and physical ideals are steps by which the spiritual ideal may be "translated" into our three-dimensional experience.

The mind builds by considering the options available for manifesting the spiritual ideal and then selects the ones to pursue (we hope, following guidance). The physical would be the carrying out of those choices and would become the result, *the experience of the spiritual ideal* as manifested. Take a few minutes to fill in these parts of the Ideals diagram, Figure 2. You may want to use a pencil, as you will likely find your ideals may take a few weeks to stabilize. (They are unlikely ever to stabilize completely, as there is no end to our growing.) The lines dividing the outer circles into quadrants are provided in case you would like to consider up to four different *areas* of your life, such as home, family and friends, education, career, physical body, hobbies, the larger community, etc. Use whichever four areas are currently most important to you.

For the purpose of meditation, we'll be focusing on the *spiritual* ideal, getting in touch with how it feels and with its inner meanings.

As mentioned above, my personal spiritual ideal is the Christ, as Christ and Love, to me, are synonymous. The more I meditate, the more I become Christ-like—as Cayce said, "here a little, there a little, line upon line, pre-

... the most important experience of this or any individual entity is to first know what *is* the ideal—spiritually. 357-13

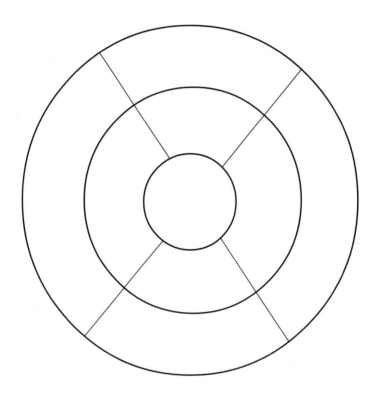

Figure 2: Setting the Ideal

cept by precept," slowly evolving closer and closer to the state of Christ Consciousness. It may take many, many years or many lifetimes, but the important point is, I am moving in this direction.

Let me now share with you a personal story that allowed me to experience firsthand the pure love of the Christ Spirit. It was the occasion of my first, true spiritual awakening, although I did not realize it at the time. The event occurred about two weeks before discovering the Edgar Cayce material that put me solidly on the spiritual path.

I was sound asleep when, at 2:00 a.m., a vividly bright, almost blinding, flash of light occurred in the doorway of my bedroom. I saw this flash of light with my mind's eye, as I was deep in the sleep state. I bolted up to a sitting position in bed and looked toward the doorway. It was dark. The flash had lasted only a fraction of a second. I saw nothing, but the warmth and love I experienced were incredible. I had never been exposed to anything like it in my entire life. I knew someone or something had caused that flash of light. It was all so poignantly real! I felt I was wrapped in a cocoon of pure love. In fact, I was so relaxed and comfortable that I simply lay back down and went to sleep.

Later, after I discovered the Cayce philosophy (which was the culmination of a twelve-year search), I realized what had happened to me. I have absolutely no doubt whatsoever that I personally experienced a visit from the Christ Light on that most eventful and significant night. The incident made an indelible impression on my memory, and I can recall the event as if it were yesterday.

4

Other Aids in Meditating

The second most important step to take in preparing for meditation is to always call upon the Christ Light for protection as we enter into the Silence. Why do we need protection? I have studied the Cayce readings, the Rosicrucian work, the Theosophical Society's work, and many other metaphysical writings, and they are in close agreement about life on the "other" side. When we die or make our return transition to Spirit, we take with us the consciousness we have built in this lifetime, which has been added to the consciousness we have built in all our other lifetimes in the earth. Jesus said in John 14:2, "In my Father's house are many mansions" (many states and levels of consciousness or awareness). Whatever state of consciousness in which we find ourselves at our transition is our "mansion," so to speak. If we are an SOB when we die, we will be an SOB in the spirit world. Death does not automatically elevate us to the status of angelic, loving beings. We create our own status in the afterlife by the lifestyles we have expressed in our current earth life.

So, when we meditate, we become Light transmitters sending God's Energy and Light into the world. If we were sufficiently sensitive or psychic when observing those who meditate, we would be able to see a glowing light, energy, or luminescence around meditators who are in the Silence.

When we are "glowing" in this way, we want to be sure to attract, not the SOBs we were just talking about (unless their intent is to be aided by the Light, of course), but beings of Light who will help us be more aware of the Love and the will of God.

The Cayce readings state that our purpose and motivation for any of our actions are the real controlling influences in our lives. If we establish a positive spiritual ideal or if our intent is to become a better person (more loving, etc.), then the intent is very good protection. When we also surround ourselves with the protective Light of the Christ Spirit, we are asking for and receiving a perfect shielding and can then safely open ourselves to the "Unseen Forces" (Cayce's term for the influences of Spirit upon our lives).

An additional word of caution here. Those who are manic-depressive or who have other serious psychological problems and may be on medication should not attempt meditation except under the guidance of a psychiatrist or a very experienced and knowledgeable meditator. It is my understanding that such psychological conditions can be made worse by meditation.

The following prayer was developed from several Cayce readings, some for the Prayer Healing Group (281 series), some for the original study group (262 series), and some for individuals (such as 257). It is my adaptation of different versions found throughout the readings. I use it myself in my personal meditations and when I am leading a group meditation:

> As we open our hearts and minds to the unseen forces that surround the throne of grace, mercy, beauty, and might, we throw about ourselves the protection found in the love of God-Consciousness, in the thought of the Christ-Consciousness.

In reading 262-19, Cayce was asked to expand on the meaning and purpose of the above statement or prayer. He responded by forcefully saying, "These expand by doing it! That's the best expansion!" So, rather than getting into the meanings and purposes, it is apparently best to *do* it, and the understanding comes using this prayer. As we strengthen our muscles by using them, in a like manner we expand the effectiveness of this prayer by using it. Some meditators add the following lines to the prayer:

> The Light of God surrounds us. The Love of God enfolds us. The Power of God protects us. The presence of God watches over us. Wherever we are, God is. And we manifest our good now.

For those of you not of the Christian faith, it may be helpful to know that the Cayce readings occasionally replace the terms *Christ* and *Christ Consciousness* with *Messiah* and *God Consciousness*. Actually, the Hebrew word *Messiah* (*Mashiyach*, Daniel 9:25) and the Greek word *Christos* both mean the same thing: *Anointed One*.

Apparently, we may call on this sanctified consciousness, which enables us to enter into a protected state during our deep meditations.

Meditation opens a channel for Energy to flow from the inner realms to the outer ones. We need to be sure we're open at the *God* end and sealed against the kind of interference we spoke of at the beginning of the chapter, but also open at the *earth* end, so the energy will have some place to go. Why not just keep it for ourselves? Energy that does not move stagnates and eventually results in discomfort. Also, God's concern is for *all* of his children. What He gives you is not for yourself alone, but for the world (your little corner of it). Some of the Energy will, of course, stay with us, but we also need to be constantly open to sharing God's energy with others. The Cayce readings admonish us to be not just good, but good for something above and beyond ourselves. Let me share with you a few readings about this:

> . . . Let the meditation end ever with these thoughts, but in the entity's own words:
> *Lord, use me in the way and manner I may be a better channel and of a greater service to Thee in the earth, now.* 4023-1

> . . . let these thoughts be oft in thy meditation and prayer:
> *Use me, O God, in the way Thou seest that I can serve Thee and Thy Cause in the earth the better.* 3395-1

> . . . let the meditation be:
> *Use me, O God, in the way and manner Thou seest that I may better serve that purpose for which I came into this experience.* 2348-2

Let this thy prayer and meditation be, morning,
noon and night:
    . . . *May I be a channel of blessings to someone in
the name of Him that promised to be—and to give—
that* [which] *we would ask in His name.* 709-1

And finally:

(Q) [307]: How may we have the mind of Christ?
(A) As we open our hearts, our minds, our souls,
that we may be a channel of blessings to others, so
may we have the mind of the Christ, who took upon
Himself the burden of the world. So may we, in our
own little sphere, take upon ourselves the burdens
of the world. The *joy*, the peace, the happiness, that
may be ours is in *doing* for the *other* fellow. For,
gaining an understanding of the laws as pertain to
right living in all its phases makes the mind in attune with *Creative* Forces, which *are* of *His* consciousness. So may we have *that* consciousness, by
putting into action *that* we know. 262-3

Now, consider the use of prayer as part of our preparation for meditation. Prayer helps purify, cleanse, and
prepare the mind for the Silence of the meditation. You
may use any kind of prayer that feels right and comfortable to you. The Cayce readings recommend the Lord's
Prayer because it is a prayer of preparation, purification,
and cleansing. It fills the bill for our needs. It contains
praise, forgiveness, and humility, and (metaphysically
interpreted) says just about everything one needs to say
in a prayer. In Chapter 6, I will describe the use of the
Lord's Prayer as an aid to raising the energy through the
chakras.
I also recommend an interpretation of the Lord's
Prayer by Emmet Fox. It is available as a pamphlet and

can be obtained through DeVorss and Co., Publishers, P.O. Box 550, Marina del Rey, CA 90294-0550. I highly recommend Emmet Fox's works, for he was one of the truly remarkable and knowledgeable metaphysicians of our times.

Prayer is talking to God. Meditation is listening to God and getting in tune with Him and His desires and direction for us. Prayer helps prepare the way for a good meditation, but the most important thing about prayer is sincerity, our attitude, and our motive and purpose for meditating. Prayer can be a special or unusual feeling, and words may not be necessary. Many times when I am about to meditate, I feel no need for formal prayer with words spoken either aloud or mentally. I have been involved with the practice of meditation for enough years that, often, my feelings dictate my actions when I begin to meditate. When I find myself in this *feeling* mode, I go to my meditation chair, sit down, and quickly slip into the Silence with no preparation beyond the prayer of protection. This was not true in my early years of meditation. It is a facility one develops with the daily practice of meditating.

There are other things we can do both physically and mentally to enhance meditation.

In purifying the body, we embrace both short-range and long-range actions. With the emphasis today concerning diet and health, no expert needs to tell us to be more aware of our weight, our nutritional habits, and the physical exercise of the body. A lighter, healthier body raises the body's vibrations and aids meditation considerably. Conversely, if we desire to obtain a healthier body, then the meditation energy will aid us; each helps the other, and they are most complementary to one another.

Fasting is an effective spiritual discipline; it gives us the opportunity to use the mind in ignoring our hunger and making the effort to pay more attention to the spirit. It can also aid us in cleansing toxins from the body. Drinking water is allowed during a true fast. There are easier, less severe fasts, such as a juice fast, during which one drinks any kind or amount of juice desired, but leaves off solid food. This gives the stomach something to digest and helps get rid of that gurgling, empty, hungry feeling that always occurs during a fast. One can go on a meat fast (no meat), a sugar fast (nothing sweet ingested), or a fat fast (no foods containing fat calories). In my opinion, a pure fast of only water is the best, most effective method for the purpose of enhancing our bodies and meditations.

For detoxifying, though, the Cayce readings offer a very effective three-day fast of eating nothing but raw apples (as many as you desire) and drinking only water during the fast. (For varieties of apple, he recommended only Jonathan, Red Delicious, Oregon Red, and Arkansas Black.) The pectin in the apples throws off any toxicity found in the body. At the completion of the fast, it is recommended that you drink a quarter cup of olive oil to complete the detoxification. I have been on this apple fast a number of times and find the first day and a half to be the most difficult part, due to the hunger encountered. Once the midway point is reached, however, I find the body has gotten the message and the balance of the fast is quite easy to accomplish. In fact, I often feel I could easily continue the fast a few more days because I am simply no longer hungry.

A word of caution here. *No one* should go on even a twenty-four-hour fast without first checking with a doctor. A fast for a diabetic person or a hypoglycemic person can be dangerous.

Fasting does, however, enhance meditation. In my case, meditations are much better than normal, as the silent period seems to be amplified, heightened, and deepened—thereby making the meditation much more enjoyable and giving me a greater sense of accomplishment. Regarding exercise, any kind is acceptable, according to one's preference. The Cayce readings indicate the best overall exercise is walking. Health research confirms this conclusion. For me, walking is my preference. Again, one should use common sense when it comes to physical exercise and check with a doctor if any questions arise regarding health or physical condition. Moderate exercise is all that is recommended here.

The Edgar Cayce readings also suggest a couple of exercises to aid in properly relaxing before meditation. The first is done while sitting and is called the *head-and-neck exercise*. While sitting in the chair you have selected for your meditation, drop your head forward in a slow, relaxed manner and then raise it back to its normal position. Do this three times. Next, slowly drop or lean your head to the rear, bringing it back to the upright position. Do this three times. Then, tilt your head toward your right shoulder, stretching it a bit, returning it then to the upright position. Do this three times. Repeat this same movement to your left three times. Finally, lower your head forward and roll it to the right 360 degrees very, very slowly until three rotations have been completed; repeat this movement to the left three times. These movements should be done *very* slowly to receive the desired benefit and require about one and one-half to two minutes to perform. According to the Cayce readings, the head-and-neck exercise aids the body in opening up the passageway through the throat chakra (thyroid gland) to help the energy raised in meditation reach the upper chakras, located in the head (pineal and pituitary glands). This exercise, done at least twice daily, will also aid your eyesight and can reduce or possibly eliminate the need for corrective lenses.

Cayce also suggests a special breathing exercise designed to open up the energy passageway and to permit the intake of oxygen to stimulate the pineal and pituitary glands. With the left forefinger, close the left nostril and breathe deeply through the right nostril, exhaling through the mouth. Do this three times. Then, with the right nostril closed, breathe in through the left nostril, and exhale through the right nostril while holding the left nostril closed, taking three breaths in this fashion.

Following this special breathing exercise, begin to breathe very slowly and very deeply, drawing in as much air into your lungs as possible. This is called *diaphragm breathing* and gets air into the lower lobes of the lungs, which usually does not occur during normal breathing. Deep breathing slows everything down in our bodies, including heart rate, and supplies more oxygen for the blood, helping us to stay more alert while we are in the Silence.

It is suggested we sit in an upright position in a comfortable chair, feet flat on the floor and hands either folded in our laps or resting on our thighs. Lying down is permitted, but the readings remark that it is easy to go to sleep in a prone position. Sitting upright helps to reduce this tendency and keeps us more alert to what is happening in the Silence. However, the physical position used while meditating is a personal choice; each of us should use the position that feels the most comfortable. The readings say it is important to keep the spine straight, as this is the pathway of the rising creative energy during meditation.

The use of an affirmation just prior to entering the Silence helps our concentration and the ability to eventually reach a *nonthinking* state of mind. Have you ever tried to blank your mind and not think any thought? It is very difficult to do, but it is the state we are attempting to reach in meditation. It is a state of Oneness, Love, and Silence impossible to put into words. All I can say is that it is a feeling you will recognize, without a shadow of a doubt, once you experience it. It is a Oneness that melds us with each expression of Energy and life in the universe; a Love all-pervading. Although it sounds like an oxymoron, the Silence is deafening, but glorious to hear—or I should say *experience*.

Let me clarify what I mean by the phrase "the Silence is deafening." When we meditate consistently, the Silence (which, of course, is normally silent), occasionally makes itself known emphatically as a *sound*, one that is very loud, so loud we cannot mistake it. Yet, while being aware of this sound of the Silence, we can still hear normal outside sounds and noises simultaneously. The sound of the Silence is similar to tinnitus (a ringing in the ear), but is not disturbing as is tinnitus. It is a comforting sound that we recognize as the Silence and that clearly reminds us of our God-Self. It rarely lasts more than thirty seconds or so. More will be said about the Silence in the next chapter.

Concerning the use of an affirmation when entering the Silence, let me clarify its importance. Cayce's readings frequently use the phrase, "Spirit is the life, mind is the builder, and the physical is the result." The readings connect this statement with the truth that we are spiritual beings living in the three-dimensional earth plane as spirit, mind, and body. Therefore, Cayce's readings suggest saying our selected affirmation (either mentally or audibly) three times—once for the Spirit, once for the mind, and once for the body—as we prepare to enter the Silence. The purpose of meditation, as we will see in the next chapter, is to attune our physical and mental bodies to their spiritual source. Repeating the affirmation three times helps us do just that.

An additional purpose and use for an affirmation upon entering the Silence is that the essence of the affirmation itself will begin to manifest in our lives the more we use it for our meditations. I have seen these essences clearly come about in my own life using the various affirmations (which really are a form of prayer) given in the *Search for God* books. For example, *Book I* covers the subjects of cooperation, knowing oneself, faith, patience, virtue, understanding, etc. When the related affirmations are used in conjunction with daily meditations, the corresponding attributes begin to manifest in our lives. We become more cooperative with the God within, our families, our neighbors, our friends, and with ourself; we begin to know and understand ourself as we are known and understood by the God within us; we see our faith become stronger; we experience more patience with ourself and others; we begin to manifest a more virtuous life, gaining more understanding of our neighbors.

If we want to increase our patience and our faith in our lives, we should ask God to help us in this regard in our prayer time prior to entering the meditative state. Some people think patience and faith will be handed them on a silver platter, but that is rarely, if ever, the case. In order for us to increase these attributes in our lives, we are given many opportunities to use patience and faith by the everyday occurrences of living and working with others. A trying person or situation in life may confront us in order for us to practice patience or faith, thereby developing these attributes by applying them in our daily living. Muscles in our bodies atrophy if not used. We develop larger biceps by pumping iron. In a like manner, spiritual qualities are developed in our lives by use and practice. What meditation does is attract to us the appropriate conditions to help us manifest specific attributes in our lives.

As an example, let me share with you a few stories to illustrate some of the fruits of my growing in faith— through meditation, affirmation, and, of course, by *applying* faith.

The first event occurred in the late 1960s, when my wife became pregnant. She experienced an early-term miscarriage and needed a curettement to be performed in a hospital. At the time, I was unemployed. We had just purchased a new home, and our money supply was critical, to say the least. We had about $50 in our checking account, no savings at the time, and no medical insurance. I was concerned as to how I was going to pay the hospital, even though she was scheduled to be there for only one day and the bill would be minimal.

The day before taking her to the hospital, I went into a special meditation to seek guidance about what I should do. About an hour after completing the meditation, I was given the strong and distinct impression to have the faith that God was with me, to take a blank check with me, and to offer to pay whatever the hospital required as we checked her in. I had the clear and comforting feeling that all would be well and that somehow there would be sufficient funds to cover any check I was asked to write.

When we arrived, I walked up to the hospital business check-in office and very confidently told them I had no insurance, but that I was willing to make the required deposit. Much to my surprise, the clerk told me not to be concerned, that I could just come by when my wife checked out the next day and settle up. The following day, I again went to pay the bill with my blank check. The clerk was very nice and informed me that they were undergoing a conversion to a new computer system and that they would send me a bill at a later date. I don't know about you, but it was the first and only time I have ever gotten in and out of a hospital without paying before the patient was allowed to go home. Six weeks later, I received the bill in the mail, exactly one day after I had received my first paycheck from my new job. (It had taken me longer to find work than I had anticipated.) Needless to say, my faith had grown considerably.

A second event took place in the early 1970s—one much more emotionally painful and traumatic. I was executive vice-president and educational coordinator for a company and owned twenty percent of the stock. The president of the company was a very nice and likable person, but he and I did not agree on the way the business was conducted. To my thinking, certain things were being done with which I strongly disagreed. The details are not important to this story. I was making good money with the company and enjoyed my work. The problems were a concern to me and, being in my early forties, I was not eager to walk away from this opportunity. I prayed and meditated for a year concerning my dilemma before receiving the guidance to resign from the company. I had another job to go to, but it was not in my field of data processing. I left the company in January 1970, and began work in the new job. But it simply was not my cup of tea, and I left after a couple of months. By this time, a severe economic recession had set in. I had more than twenty years' experience in my profession, but I was also forty-two years old. Due to the recession and my age, I failed to find work in my field. My credit was good, and we were able to survive the year by borrowing heavily. My wife found the stress very difficult, and we divorced in early 1971.

This was the most traumatic part of my upcoming five-year period of unemployment. I did not want the divorce, nor did I want to become a part-time father to our three-year-old son. We had to sell our home and the 125 acres of land, in which we had invested for later use, in order to meet the never-ending financial obligations. During the next five years, I became a jack-of-all-trades. I mowed lawns, painted houses, worked as a carpenter's helper, ran a self-service gas station, and sold portable buildings, mobile homes, and any other thing I could find to sell. I became a gardener for a local cemetery, trimming grass away from the tombstones and the grave markers. I took any job I could find to hold body and soul together and to meet my obligations.

It was a most educational experience. I met many very interesting people. My 14-year-old son from a previous marriage came to live with me, and I learned he was involved with drugs. In 1974, I developed high blood pressure (Was it any wonder?). I became a master at manipulating funds with the several credit cards I had obtained while solvent. I often borrowed money on one card to make a payment on another. Believe it or not, I was never late with a credit card payment or a personal loan payment during that entire period of unemployment. Many of my metaphysical friends came to my aid and helped out as they could. I never earned more than $1,000 a year for the next five years, after being used to a comfortable, five-digit income. You could say it was a confining and restricting, but most educational, experience.

However, I had encounters and happenings of a positive nature that might not have occurred otherwise. I learned the true value of money and material possessions. I found I could survive on far less than I ever thought possible. All of my priorities changed, and I discovered a peace, patience, and faith I had never before experienced nor considered likely. In short, it was, without a doubt, the most interesting, positive, challenging, provocative, faith-building set of lesson-learning episodes ever to occur in my life. I am most thankful for the opportunities given me to gain the wisdom, the knowledge, and the faith garnered through those once-in-a-lifetime circumstances. I was often asked by friends and acquaintances why I seemed to be so calm and serene under such adverse, traumatic circumstances. I recall telling them I felt it was the meditation Energy constantly guiding me that kept me calm and kept me from becoming panic-stricken. I was doing everything I knew to do in taking whatever job I found, but my most important action was asking God for His help and direction each and every day.

The following experience is another example of the protection and guidance I received:

I had borrowed more than $10,000 on a personal, 360-day note. When it was up for payment or renewal, I again found myself lacking that amount of money. I had about a week before the note was due, so again I held a special meditation for the express purpose of receiving some guidance as to what I should do. Nothing came to me during or immediately after the meditation. Yet, on the day before I was to pay the note, I got a clear feeling I should go to the bank, discuss the situation with the loan officer, and ask for a year's extension. After receiving this clairsentient guidance, I felt reassured and calm, knowing I could get that extension.

The next day, I bravely walked up to the loan officer responsible for this loan and explained to him that my cash flow would be seriously impaired if I paid the note off. Could he give me a year's extension of the note, at which time I should have no cash flow problem, as my home was up for sale and should be sold by that time? He graciously consented, probably because he had known me and my father for a number of years and knew of our integrity. Exactly thirty days before the loan's due date, I was able to sell our home, which provided me with the necessary funds to pay off the note and the $1,500 in accumulated interest.

In another example, two high school friends of mine knew of my situation and let me rent one of their rental houses (a three-bedroom, two-bath brick home) for a third of the normal rent. It was in the country on one acre of land. I was able to have a vegetable garden. Here, I communed with nature in a serene, calm setting, and I began to heal. I lived there until I finally found permanent employment in my field. Many people came to my aid during this difficult time, and I quickly found out who my real friends were.

I could cite other examples of such loving guidance and providence, but the foregoing should be sufficient. By the time this five-year period was over, my faith muscles were bulging. I consider this stage of my life to have been the most spiritually productive ever to occur. Although there have been other spiritual growth times during my seventy-plus years in the earth this time around, none has been as prolific in terms of positive lessons as this one. At times, it was painful, but it was never dull and always educational. I call it my *Joshua experience* (a term I will explain later).

In this chapter, I have covered a number of procedures in preparing for meditation, but let me repeat the two most important steps: Set your spiritual ideal, and surround yourself with the Christ Light.

5

The Heart of Meditation

*I*f you were to ask 100 meditators to define meditation and explain the way they perceive and practice it, you might easily get 100 varied answers. Their replies would depend on the material they have read and studied on the subject, along with their understanding of that material and their experience with it. Therefore, from my point of view, there is no such thing as a one-and-only way to meditate, just as there is no one-and-only true religion, regardless of arguments to the contrary. Truth is Truth, wherever one may find it. If the Edgar Cayce readings are correct, the soul will recognize spiritual

Truth, regardless of its outer form.

What, then, is meditation? Webster says it is "continued thought; reflection; specifically religious contemplation," and I do not disagree with this definition, but simply say meditation is much more. The meditation discipline also includes prayer, even though prayer and meditation are not the same thing. Prayer is talking to God, and meditation is listening for His answers and direction. This, however, is an over-simplification. The essence of meditation is the *Silence*, which will be discussed later. Edgar Cayce gave the best definition of meditation that I have found in my extensive research:

> It is not musing, not daydreaming; but as ye find your bodies made up of the physical, mental and spiritual, it is the attuning of the mental body and the physical body to its spiritual source . . .
>
> Then, it (meditation) is the attuning of thy physical and mental attributes seeking to know the relationships to the Maker. *That* is true meditation. 281-41

In the fortieth chapter of *The Aquarian Gospel of Jesus the Christ*, Jesus gives a very detailed account of what meditation is all about:

> And Jesus said, There is a Silence where the soul may meet its God, and there the fount of wisdom is, and all who enter are immersed in light, and filled with wisdom, love and power . . . The Silence is not circumscribed; is not a place closed in with wall, or rocky steeps, nor guarded by the sword of man . . . Men carry with them all the time the secret place where they meet their God . . . It matters not where men abide, on mountain top, in deepest vale, in marts of trade, or in the quiet home; they may at

once, at any time, fling wide the door, and find the Silence, find the house of God; it is within the soul . . . And when life's heavy load is pressing hard, it is far better to go out and seek a quiet place to pray and meditate . . . The Silence is the kingdom of the soul which is not seen by human eyes. When in the Silence, phantom forms may flit before the mind; but they are all subservient to the will; the master soul may speak and they are gone . . . If you would find this Silence of the soul, you must yourself prepare the way. None but the pure in heart may enter here . . . And you must lay aside all tenseness of the mind, all business cares, all fears, all doubts and troubled thoughts. Your human will must be absorbed by the Divine; then you will come into a consciousness of holiness.

This is a logical and realistic description of the meditation practice and process from the Master Himself, and one with which I quite agree from my own experience.

Now we have reviewed what Webster, Cayce, and Jesus said about meditation. Let me add what I believe meditation is, after having engaged in the practice for more than thirty-five years. Meditation is a stilling process: letting go and letting God direct our lives; involving ourselves in the quietness of Spirit; "plugging in" to recharge our batteries, so to speak, to obtain all the energy we may need in our daily living—not only physical energy, but mental and spiritual Energy. It is an attuning process. Finally, it is the offering of ourselves as a channel or instrument through which God can fully express His love in this world.

Consider this: If, as the Cayce readings say, we have the spark of the Divine within us and are a part of the Godhead; and if we, humankind, are the highest expression of God in this earth, having dominion over the animals, plants, and minerals; if we have been given the free will to accept Him or reject Him, to express His love or not, to let the higher God-nature come through, or to let the lower selfish nature come through—then, doesn't it make sense that God needs us to become one with Him in consciousness and expression in order for His love to be fully manifested through us? I suggest it is up to us, as individual soul expressions of God, to choose to become one with Him. When we do this, we will gain love and peace within ourselves.

We come now to the most important part of the meditation process, the Silence. (As you may have noted, I capitalize the words Silence, Energy, and Light throughout this book, because those words, the way I am using them, represent the God within us. Some might disagree with my use of the word *Silence*, but that is when and where we make the contact with the God within.)

This is the area of meditation most difficult to master, but most rewarding to the meditator. This is where the movement of Energy takes place; where the chakras or psychic centers are cleansed; where the spiritual ideal begins to respond to the Energy manifesting more and more in the life of the meditator; where, ultimately, one will come to that point of Silence and Light that only the individual person can fully experience and understand. I am not referring to seeing with the mind's eye the flashes of light that often occur in the Silence. I speak of the Silence and Light alluded to earlier that cannot be put into words by those who have had such an experience. It may require many years to reach this point—indeed, perhaps many more lifetimes. Do not let this statement deter you from pursuing such an encounter; the rewards along the way are many and wonderful to behold. Within six months (or less for many people), you will see positive changes in your actions, disciplines, and attitudes, which will amaze you and encourage you to "keep on keeping on" with the daily meditation effort.

When you enter into the Silence, following the use of an affirmation suited to you, Energy begins to move up from the root chakra or gonads (see Figure 1 on page 9). This Energy moves through the other six chakras, stimulating them and cleansing them of the negativity and misuse to which we may have willfully subjected them in this lifetime or the many others we have lived in the earth. This Energy ultimately manifests through our spiritual ideal, whatever it may be; thus, the importance of the chosen ideal being of a positive nature. Recall that the Energy does not care how it is used. Energy is impersonal. As water is symbolic of Spirit in the earth, the Energy is like water in that water seeks its lowest level unless it is directed and controlled by dams, pumps, canals, etc. In a like manner, the Energy that rises during meditation seeks the level of consciousness of the meditator. Remember the rudderless ship mentioned in a previous chapter? As we meditate, it is imperative that we have established an uplifting, positive ideal in order that the energy may be directed according to our conscious choice.

The seven chakras (Figure 1) are divided into two groups, according to the Edgar Cayce readings. The first four chakras—the gonads, the cells of Leydig, the adrenals, and the thymus—are the four lower or earth chakras. The other three chakras, the thyroid/parathyroid, the pineal, and the pituitary are the upper, mental/spiritual chakras. Keep in mind, the seven chakras are also called psychic or spiritual centers and are associated with the endocrine glands. There are other chakras in and around the body, but these seven are the most important in our study of meditation. They all have other names found in Eastern lore, and those names will be given as I discuss each chakra. I do not want to get too technical in my presentation of this material, as I have observed that many students who have done so miss the real value of meditation. It is easy to get so hung up in the mechanics, techniques, and ceremonial aspects of this practice that you lose the spirit of what we are trying to accomplish. To repeat, I must stress the importance of one's motive and purpose for learning to meditate. Nothing can replace the sincerity and desire to know the Truth that can set us free.

As stated before, the Silence is the most profound part of meditation, the heart and soul of the process. It can be nebulous, mysterious, inexplicable, confidential, intimate, personal, abstruse, or subjective—or all of the above. Many people, especially novice meditators, might have a tendency to expect some kind of *experience* or *vision* during the Silence. While this may happen during the Silence, it is not what we are seeking. Remember, there are many methods and techniques of meditating. The technique presented here is from the Edgar Cayce readings and my personal experience. Meditation can be used for many things. I am proposing we use it for a better, closer connection to our Source, our ever-present taproot of Energy, our infallible guidance system, our highway markers for life's direction. A reliable affirmation for anyone entering the Silence is found in Psalm 46:10: "Be still, and know that I *am* God." In attempting to explain the power of this statement, I would punctuate it with a couple of extra commas:

Be still, and know, that I am, God.

Let me give my reasons for the additional commas by explaining the "I am" portion of the verse. When Moses was on the mountaintop and he asked God by what name He should be called, God answered, "I am that I am." When I first read this in the Bible as a young man, I thought this was a stupid answer. (Obviously, I did not understand the statement.) Many years later, during my studies of the Cayce readings and other metaphysical writings, I began to understand what was meant by the "I am that I am" message. I explain it in the following way in my seminars on meditation. If God is all-powerful and ever-present as we are taught, if our souls are literally sparks of His Divine Being and we carry that part of Him wherever we go and however we manifest ourselves, then the statement is a personal one to each of us as individual expressions of the Godhead. At this point in seminars, I point to a woman in the front row and emphatically exclaim, "I am *that* I am," making sure to time my pointing gesture to coincide with the word *that*. I repeat this with the man sitting next to her and with a few other participants. Another way to interpret the "I am that I am" statement is: I am that I am which is within me and which is (a part of) God Himself, that spark of the Divine within each soul.

Again, look at Psalm 46:10. When we say "Be still, and know, that I am, God," we mean, "Be Still (quiet the body and the mind and listen), and know (really become acquainted with Him on a personal level), that I am (the *I am* within me), (which we call) God." With this interpretation and understanding of verse 46:10, the affirmation takes on a whole new meaning and power: It becomes our prayer and our desire to make meaningful contact with the Spirit within us. I recommend to beginning meditators that they use this affirmation exclusively for the first few weeks. It not only has a great deal of power, but it also is short and easy to remember when our minds begin to wander in the Silence.

It is not unusual, during a ten- or fifteen-minute period of Silence, for one's mind to wander and for normal thinking processes to intrude dozens of times. We will find ourselves thinking everyday thoughts of what we should do about Johnny's school lunch tomorrow or what time our spouse's flight is coming in next Monday or what food to prepare for the upcoming party, etc. When this occurs and we become aware we are *thinking* rather than stilling the mind to a nonthinking state, we need to restate the affirmation and recenter our mind.

Another excellent technique for stilling the mind is to focus our attention upon our breathing. Focusing on our breathing gives the mind something to hold onto during the Silence. I cannot think of anything more representative of the God within us than our breath. We cannot keep the physical body going without breathing. It is not something to which we normally give any attention. *What* makes us breathe? Is it not the Spirit within us? Don't we stop breathing when we die and our souls leave our bodies?

The key to successful meditation is to control our minds, make connection with the Spirit within us, and go deep into ourselves. Let me point out Jesus' statement on meditation in the fortieth chapter of the *Aquarian Gospel* in verse 11, "When in the Silence, phantom forms may flit before the mind; but they are all subservient to the will; the master soul may speak and they are gone." It is *our* will He speaks of and *we* are the master souls that speak. I am in my thirty-fifth year of meditating and still frequently have trouble with my mind wandering. So, do not be discouraged. It takes persistent work, dedication, and effort to get the mind to be still.

Many people describe to me the beautiful visions and past-life memories they have during the Silence. I tell them these are images from the subconscious mind that are distracting them from the meditation discipline. When such visions and pictures occur, we should simply make note of them, set them gently aside, and return to the affirmation or focus on our breathing.

The deeper we go into the Silence the better, for this is

where the real spiritual renewal and growth take place. Many people have undisciplined minds. The unchecked conscious mind leads us around and controls us. But there comes a time to assert our authority and our will as free-willed and free-thinking individuals. In time, the meditation effort and discipline will do just that.

When a problem or situation needs a solution, we should take it into meditation with prayer. We are not trying to get an answer during the Silence. We leave the problem with the God within, and we receive the answer later as a result of our meditation effort. If we are fortunate, the answer might come in a day or two. Or it may take weeks or even months. But the answer will come in normal, everyday ways, such as a letter in the mail; a knock on the door from a friend, family member, or even a stranger; a telephone call; an intuitive or inspirational thought or a dream. I have experienced clairaudience only four or five times in my many years of meditation. This is riveting when it happens, but getting an answer in this way happens only rarely. Meditation makes us more alert to the everyday situations mentioned above. I will share with you in a later chapter how I was able to quit a twenty-six year cigarette-smoking habit using the guidance and Energy from meditation.

It is not uncommon for meditators to go to sleep during the Silence. Do not be discouraged when this occurs; the Cayce readings say this can happen to anyone who meditates, especially when physically tired or mentally drained. In time, sleep will occur infrequently, and a deeper experience will be yours. What better way to go to sleep than while attempting meditation? The Cayce readings suggest we should sit up straight in a comfortable chair because we are not as likely to go to sleep in a sitting position as we are in a prone position. (I prefer the sitting position since I nearly always fall asleep when lying down.)

There is a possibility of leaving the body while in deep meditation. I have on a number of occasions, but that is never my intention. When I leave my body, I am not aware of it. I do not know where I go or what I do. It is not important to me. I have yet to bring back to my conscious memory anything that happened to me while in such a state. It just seems to be something that happens from time to time during the meditation process. I rather suspect it is similar to leaving our bodies while we sleep. The Cayce readings indicate almost all of us leave our bodies almost every night during sleep. It is the soul's time to review what we have done during the day. We may also visit others for various reasons. I have had a few people report that they have awakened during the night to find me standing at the foot of their bed. I have never been aware of these visits. I can only assume my visit was for the purpose of aiding them in some way or perhaps to learn something from them. The soul does not sleep. Only the physical body requires sleep.

The question has been raised as to how I know I have left my body during certain rare meditations since, as I have stated, I do not remember where I have been or what I may have done during such an experience. I cannot give any scientific evidence for such an event of course, but I will attempt to explain it in a manner that will make it understandable and believable. I have often fallen asleep during my meditations. I can tell that I have done so because I wake myself up with my snoring or what I call "breath snortling," and I always have that "I've been asleep" feeling, along with the associated sleepiness in my eyes. However, when I have had those rare out-of-body experiences during meditation, the coming back to conscious awareness is a vastly different happening. First of all, I am jolted out of the Silence, as if I have jumped into or been shoved back into my body, with a definite alertness or acute awareness. And frequently, though not always, I have experienced a "time distortion" event along with it. (Time distortion is explained in the next chapter.) It is an unusual alertness/awareness that is a clearly defined, distinct, and unmistakable vivacity of spirit.

Remember, we are not trying to get information on a conscious level or to have a vision or an experience during the Silence. Anything of that nature of which we have need will be provided as a result of our meditation effort. Some people have the idea that they will hear bells and whistles or see visions and have great revelations during the Silence. Any information, guidance, or experiences we may need will come *outside* of the meditation process as a *result* of our daily meditation.

The best advice I can give you regarding the Silence is just to let go and listen, let God have His way with you, and trust the guidance you receive during your everyday conscious state. The impersonal God is now your personal God because you made the choice to meet Him on a deep, personal level. The meditation Energy will give you a heightened awareness of what is happening around you in a way you have not recognized before. His guidance has always been there—only now you are more sensitive to it and can more easily recognize it.

Let's go over the most important part of the Silence portion of the meditation. The mind is a tough, unruly servant because we have permitted it to be that way. The most difficult point to master while in the Silence is to keep the mind as much as possible in a nonthinking state. This may sound like an oxymoron because a legitimate question from the novice meditator is, "Okay, but am I not thinking when I tell myself to blank my mind?" Yes, literally speaking, we are. This is why I suggest that we focus on our deep breathing. It is the easiest way to reach a nonthinking state.

As mentioned earlier, another method to control our

wandering thoughts is to recenter our attention on the affirmation. It eliminates indiscriminate thinking and assists in focusing on the affirmation itself which, in turn, aids in manifesting the essence of the affirmation in daily life.

I am by no means saying we cannot have beautiful and spontaneous visions or experiences during the Silence. Let me give an example. A good friend of mine, a daily meditator, described to me the beautiful angel that appeared to her during the Silence. She enjoyed the experience, made note of it, and returned to her affirmation. We discussed her experience and agreed it was a wonderful and exciting vision. Taking note of the vision and returning to her affirmation was the appropriate reaction. She might easily have concentrated on the angel and been distracted from the Silence.

The important thing is to let go of *all* mental activity and let the God within guide us, which can only happen in the Silence. Believe me, the Wisdom within knows our physical, mental, emotional, and spiritual status far, far better than we do. (I will share with you later some instances of this greater Wisdom working through me.)

When we come out of the Silence—which should take ten to fifteen minutes for beginners—we will have accumulated a great deal of God Energy. At this point, the Energy should be given away in a *healing prayer* for Mother Earth and her peoples. The Cayce readings recommend we pray for others at this time. We will have more than enough Energy left over for ourselves, following our healing prayer time. A suggested procedure is to send out the Energy and to pray for the raising of the consciousness of all mankind; for the healing of the earth; for God's work to spread throughout the world via religions, churches, spiritual organizations (such as the A.R.E.), etc.; for the homeless, the hungry, the destitute, the ill, the forlorn, the lonely, the fearful; for those whose names appear on prayer lists throughout the world; for political leaders; for family members and friends; and for whomever else we are guided to pray. Following the prayer healing time, I like to end the meditation with a prayer of thanksgiving for the many, many blessings God has bestowed upon me, the earth, and her inhabitants.

The Silence is the very heart and soul of meditation. The preparatory prayer of purification leading into the Silence, the three repetitions of an affirmation before entering the Silence, the giving away (for healing purposes) of the meditation Energy built up during the Silence—these are all important parts of the meditation exercise, but the Silence itself is what allows the Energy of God to move within us. It is also the part most difficult to master—and to describe to the beginning student. What should the student expect to feel or experience in the Silence?

Meditation—Fruits of the Spirit

When we enter the Silence, we are attempting to become very, very quiet in both body and mind. Conquering the body and its idiosyncrasies and rumblings is relatively easy; conquering the flighty, active mind is another matter. This is the reason I suggest restating verbally or mentally the affirmation used prior to entering the silence or to simply focus attention upon breathing, as such action aids the randomly thinking mind. Being able to hold our attention on either the affirmation or breathing *and to be aware that we are doing so* is one indication of being properly into the Silence. Another is becoming very comfortable with just being there; *a feeling, a true knowing* that we are there. Eventually, we will begin to experience a loss of awareness of where we are and what we are doing, a state similar to the alpha or theta state of brain wave activity. This is deep meditation and a state we are attempting to reach every time we meditate. Such a state may be reached only occasionally; do not expect it to happen every time. The silence is melding and blending our outer selves to the God-Self within. This I believe, is what Cayce meant in his definition of what meditation is, i.e.; " . . . it is the attuning of the mental body and the physical body to its spiritual source." (281-41)

Further support concerning the importance of meditation and of the Silence itself comes from Neale Donald Walsch's book, *Conversations with God, Book 3,* wherein God remarks:

> And what is it of which you eventually become totally aware? You eventually become totally aware of Who You Are.
>
> Daily meditation is one way you may achieve this. Yet it requires commitment, dedication, a decision to seek inner experience, not outer reward.
>
> And remember, the silences hold the secrets. And so the sweetest sound is the sound of silence. This is the song of the soul.
>
> If you believe the noises of the world rather than the silences of your soul, you will be lost.

Now, let us look at some of the effects of this Energy rising through our chakras, the specific effects on the chakras themselves, and the resulting effects in our daily lives.

6

The Energy Moves Through Us

THE CLEANSING OF THE SOUL

I started to title this chapter "Cleansing the Chakras," but then I realized that, as the meditation Energy moves through us, more accurately it cleanses and purifies the *soul* of its negative memories and habit patterns. Still, it is helpful to look at the chakras as the sites where this cleansing is done when the centers are bathed in the Energy that arises during meditation.

The chakras are the contact points of the three-dimensional expression of the soul (Spirit), the mind, and the physical body. The Edgar Cayce readings indicate that the chakras relate symbolically to the seven churches (meeting places) mentioned in Revelation in the Bible. They are also the vibrational storehouses of our memory from our creation as individual soul expressions of the Godhead.

Have you ever wondered why you sometimes experience instant love or instant dislike for certain persons you meet for the first time? My in-depth study of reincarnation has convinced me that strong reactions of this kind are due to past-life experiences with those souls and that the memory of them is stored in the genes and chakras. If the former association was a bad experience, you may have some negative karma (debts) to work out with the other person. This is where meditation can assist you in dealing with the karma. Meditation cleanses these chakras over a period of time and brings forth the memory, knowledge, and wisdom needed for you to resolve the differences and to begin to forgive and love the person.

Meditation also exposes negative, self-destructive habit patterns within you that require adjusting and correcting. You are constantly meeting yourself. Anytime you have an emotional reaction of any kind, be assured you are seeing a reflection of yourself. This is why we can see others' faults quite easily. We remember them in our own soul. If we react with a negative emotion, then we are still carrying the fault we see in another and have yet to overcome it. However, if we recognize the fault and do not judge it, then we have overcome the fault recognized. We could not recognize a fault in another unless we have already experienced the fault in this or a past life.

Consider how meditation helps in identifying negative faults and memories, as illustrated by the following analogy: If you put a couple of spoonfuls of dirt in a glass of water and let it sit for a minute or two, the dirt settles to the bottom of the glass. The sediment represents the residue of misused Energy over many lifetimes. The water represents the purifying Spirit. If the glass is held under running water, the force of the water stirs up the water in the glass and agitates it, causing the sediment to rise and flow out of the glass until only clean, pure water remains.

This is similar to what happens when we meditate. The movement of Energy during meditation stirs up the negativity we have created in the past by our misuse of God's Energy. These negative effects rise to the surface of our consciousness and get our attention. However, unlike the sediment in the glass that just flushes away, we are given the opportunity to *work* with those negative faults and habits brought to our awareness. They do not just spill away. We have to work with them until they are no longer a part of our lives and soul expression. But—and a very big *but* here—we are given the required energy, guidance, and direction with this same meditation-generated Energy to correct and purify the condition, whatever it may be. I believe Paul alluded to these same conditions in his teachings when he wrote that (and I paraphrase here) *with every temptation and problem, God gives us a way of escape and the strength to deal with them.* Cor. 10:13

Following a substantial amount of soul growth, we may well find that many good things come to us and happen to us as pure gifts, with no apparent work done on our part. (Soul growth involves downs as well as ups, entailing both joy and pain and signifying karmic lessons, which is another way of saying we gain wisdom through experience.) In reality, however, positive growth is a result of turning within over a period of time, diligently and sincerely attempting to improve our ability to love ourselves as we are loved and to love others the way we would have them love us.

As to the movement of the Energy, as explained earlier, it begins at the root chakra (the gonads or sex glands) during meditation and begins to flow up through the other six chakras (See Figure 1 on page 9). The details of the flow of Energy through the various glands are not important. It is only important to realize that this movement of cleansing Energy is taking place. Most of the time, you are not consciously aware of this movement of Energy, and it is not necessary to be aware of it for it to work. I will later outline some basic effects you may experience that will let you become aware of such movement.

The first (root) chakra is where we obtain most of our bodily energies. Most of us know and have experienced the power of the sex drive and know how powerful that Energy can be. It can be used self-indulgently and selfishly, or it can be used positively, lovingly, and creatively. It is always our choice. The gonads might be likened to a motor or generator within the body. This same sexual Energy rises when we enter into the Silence. It is this procreational Energy we need and use to create physical channels through which souls may reenter the earth for spiritual growth. Use of the Energy at the gonadal level is represented by the color red, and the corresponding word that opens that chakra when we say the Lord's Prayer is *bread* (Give us this day our daily bread).

The second chakra (or gland) is in the abdominal area of the body and is connected in the Cayce readings with the Lyden gland (the cells of Leydig). According to Cayce, this gland is a part of the genital system and is also the "seat of the soul." The gland has become dormant in some persons from nonuse. Purifying this gland can greatly assist us in becoming more creative. It is represented by the color orange, and the key word in the Lord's Prayer is *temptation* (and lead us not into temptation).

The third chakra is in the area of the adrenal glands, situated atop the kidneys. It is our "fight-or-flight" gland

and is usually associated with the solar plexus. This gland gives the little eighty-five-year-old lady the strength to lift the end of an automobile off of her grandchild trapped under it. Extraordinary feats of this kind have often been reported.

On a less dramatic note, I recall a time when my adrenals kicked in forcefully. I was about thirteen years old and worked an early morning paper route. It was a dark, blustery morning, and I saw a shadow move on a porch that looked like a man in a hat and trench coat. It scared me out of my wits. I dropped my newspaper tote bag and ran at least a mile before I calmed down and logic returned. I felt as if I had covered the mile in three minutes or less. I was acutely aware of the speed I had attained during my run.

As I understand the Cayce readings, the third chakra is the seat of karmic memory. The solar plexus has often been referred to as our second brain. It is not coincidence that our "gut-feelings" are often the result of our intuition, which, in turn, might be a result of karmic memory. It is represented by the color yellow, and the Lord's Prayer word associated with it is *debts* (and forgive us our debts as we forgive our debtors).

The fourth chakra (heart chakra) relates to the thymus gland located above the heart. It physically is much larger at birth, to help develop our immunity from disease. The infant's need is greater than the adult's, since it has not had the opportunity to build its own immune defenses. It is my understanding that the thymus gland atrophies and becomes smaller as we grow older, although it continues functioning.

The heart rules the head or is itself ruled by the head via the will. It is our love center, but it can be used to do evil, of course, if we choose. As our health center, its representative color is green, which denotes healing. The key Lord's Prayer word is *evil* (but deliver us from evil).

To clarify Cayce's use of this word, let me add that the readings indicate there is no "Satan" or "devil," apart from the power given to it in man's thinking or belief systems. Cayce made it quite plain that the only real enemy or "devil" we may encounter is our own selfishness, or our lower self as opposed to our Higher [God] Self. Evil results from the negative or selfish Energy we express in our lives. So, evil is the selfish use of God's Energy, and any evil we encounter, we have created for ourselves, whether during this lifetime or a prior one. Cayce says we are constantly meeting ourselves and what we see in another is a reflection of ourselves, or else how could we recognize it? Of course, the opposite is also true: Any good we see in another is also a reflection of our own good. Therefore, if we see evil in someone, let us be reminded that it is a reflection of ourselves and choose to make no judgment of that person. When we say, in the Lord's Prayer, " . . . but deliver us from evil," we are asking God to protect us from our own selfish nature and to help us use our free will to choose the good.

The fifth chakra (throat chakra) is the thyroid and parathyroid glands. It is the center of our *will*, or will power, used to make our daily choices. I like to call it our *choice* center. It is the special place where the soul sustains its gift of free will given by the Father-Mother God. Cayce quoted this statement in many readings: "I have . . . set before thee good and evil. Choose thou whom thou will serve," (254-12), which originally comes from Deuteronomy 30:15. The color for this chakra is blue, and the key words in the Lord's Prayer are *will* and *kingdom* (Thy kingdom come, thy will be done [and] for Thine is the *kingdom* and the power and the glory).

The sixth chakra (crown chakra) is the pineal gland in the top and center of the head. It is often referred to as the Christ center or Light center. It is noteworthy that this is the one place in the body in which phosphorus is found. Phosphorus is the element used by the firefly to flash its light during the night.

Some schools of thought refer to the pineal as the third eye, but Cayce's readings indicate the seventh chakra or master gland—the pituitary—is the third eye, and I accept the Cayce readings' interpretation in this regard.

The pineal gland is important; the readings stress its connection with the Lyden gland (second chakra) and the "silver cord" extending between the two chakras. It is this *silver cord* that is broken when the body dies and the soul leaves. The color for the sixth chakra is indigo, and the key words in the Lord's Prayer are *name* and *power* (Hallowed be Thy name [and] for Thine is the kingdom and the power and the glory).

The seventh chakra, the pituitary gland (master gland), is just above and behind the bridge of the nose. It is slightly below the pineal gland. If you were to look at the body and the location of the seven chakras from a side view, you would find that an imaginary line from the first through the seventh chakras would resemble a shepherd's crook. This shepherd's crook is the "staff" in the Twenty-third Psalm, and the pituitary gland is the "cup that runneth over": 'Thy rod and Thy staff, they comfort me . . . Thou anointest my head with oil, my cup runneth over."

The cup represents the Light filling the whole body and cleansing it as a result of our steadfastness in meditation.

The pituitary gland produces many of the hormones the body requires. If this gland does not function exactly as it should (karma is relevant here), the result might affect growth, making a person unusually short or extremely tall. The gland is also instrumental in the puberty cycle. When the pituitary gland releases a special hormone, usually between the ages of twelve and fourteen, this hormone is sent through the body and stimulates the gonads (root chakra), which, in turn, produce another special hormone that returns to stimulate the pituitary, and, at this point, puberty begins.

It is the pituitary as the (third) *eye* that gave us clairvoyance millennia ago. With the exception of a few persons, this eye is no longer active in most humans, due, perhaps, to the misuse of our Energy.

The color for this chakra is violet or white, depending on your school of thought. White indicates purity here and the blending of all the known colors. The key words from the Lord's Prayer are *Father* and *glory* (Our Father which art in heaven [and] for Thine is the kingdom and the power and the glory.)

In discussing the pineal gland or sixth chakra, I remarked that it is the Christ or Light center. This same chakra is mentioned in the *Aquarian Gospel* 40:15-18:

. . . You are within the Holy Place, and you will see upon a living shrine the candle of the Lord aflame . . . And when you see it burning there, look deep within the temple of your brain, and you will see it all aglow . . . In every part, from head to foot, are candles all in place, just waiting to be lighted by the flaming torch of love . . . And when you see the candles all aflame, just look, and you will see, with eyes of soul, the waters of the fount of wisdom rushing on; and you may drink and there abide.

Verses 19 though 23 describe the opening of the seventh chakra or pituitary gland:

. . . And then the curtains part, and you are in the holiest of All, where rests the Ark of God, whose covering is the Mercy Seat . . . Fear not to lift the sacred board; the Tables of the Law are in the Ark concealed . . . Take them and read them well; for they contain all precepts and commands that men will ever need . . . And in the Ark, the magic wand of prophecy lies waiting for your hand; it is the key to all the hidden meanings of the present, future, past . . . And then, behold, the manna there, the hidden bread of life; and he who eats shall never die.

What powerful and glorious promises we are given when we attain to this level of spirituality! To me, it would be the level of Christ Consciousness we all are seeking. Verse 24 of this chapter gives us a clue as to why the attainment does not come easily:

The cherubim have guarded well for every soul this treasure box, and whosoever will may enter in and find his own.

It has been so well guarded, of course, because man has been so slow to learn his lessons of love. Man cannot be trusted with such knowledge and power until he has the wisdom to know how to properly use them.

What magnificent, wondrous promises we have to look forward to. It is all the motivation I need to "keep on keeping on."

A Moderate Movement of the Energy Is Best

A few words of caution to those who think that if a little meditation can aid in their spiritual growth, then even more can hasten their illumination. This is not necessarily so! Many people who are more idealistic and less pragmatic than those of us who have gained the wisdom of experience from our mistakes and errors may decide excessive meditation Energy can help them reach the "perfected" state in a much shorter time. They believe that if ten or fifteen minutes of meditation every day can do as much as they begin to see occurring in their lives, then obviously three or four times that amount will enhance spiritual growth even more. I made this mistake myself. I had just returned from the A.R.E. Headquarters in Virginia Beach, Virginia, in 1965, all aglow and inspired by what I had learned. Having meditated twice a day for three or four years, I had seen phenomenal changes occur in my life. I was thirty-eight at the time. My meditation sessions were about twenty-five to thirty minutes in length, with ten or fifteen minutes spent in the Silence. I felt that, with all the progress and wonderful things I was experiencing from two-a-day meditations, I could increase my growth exponentially by going to three or four meditations per day and upping my Silence to an hour each time.

I had been married a little over a year and a half, and the marriage was solid and happy. There were no problems between us, not even sexual. I had no interest at all in looking outside our marriage for companionship or sex. I was meditating three or four times a day, with three to four hours of increased Energy gained in the Silence. After about a month of this increased meditation Energy, I began to notice my sexual drive was becoming quite pronounced. I began looking upon women I did not know and upon my female business acquaintances as being particularly alluring and desirable. This was not normal for me, and to my way of thinking, there was no reason for this type of reaction on my part. It was quite disturbing. Fortunately, I did not succumb to these feelings and did not complicate my karma further. As luck would have it, my good friend and mentor, Hugh Lynn Cayce, came to town for a lecture. I was able to gain his wisdom and enlightenment concerning this matter. Hugh Lynn was the eldest son of Edgar Cayce and was, at that time, the President and Managing Director of the

A.R.E., was an avid meditator, and had much knowledge and expertise regarding meditation.

After his evening lecture, I had the opportunity to discuss my concern with him privately. I explained the events that had taken place since my return from A.R.E. Headquarters. He asked me how much I was meditating and how long I was spending in the Silence. My answer brought a paternal, knowing smile to his face as he began to help me understand the problem. He explained I had obviously misused my sexual Energy in one or more past lives and had a lot of negative energy patterns stored in my root chakra, due to the excesses. Because I was meditating beyond a safe level, with the negative traits still stored in my root chakra, the meditation Energy was working overtime to clean out my gonads. The Energy could not rise beyond the root chakra and was spinning in circles, going nowhere. Since it could not escape the gonads, the Energy tried to express itself through the natural function of the gland: sex. It was like a clogged pipe packed with dirt over a long period of time, requiring a great deal of flushing to properly clean out the dirt so water could flow freely. Hugh Lynn instructed me to back away from excessive meditation and return to my twice-a-day meditations, with the recommended ten minutes or so of Silence. I did as he instructed, and the problem went away. It was a significant educational event in my learning the values and proper uses of meditation Energy. As I have said before, the Energy is a two-edged sword and can cut both ways. We have been given the free will to direct its cutting.

Two more quick stories to stress the danger of overdoing meditation. One young man had the same idea and desire as did I. Wanting to speed up his spiritual evolution to reach the Christ Consciousness as quickly as possible, he increased his meditations far more than I did and wound up in a mental institution for six months to get straightened out. He is fine now, but it was a valuable and costly lesson for him. Another young man also increased his meditation period to a high level and became mentally unbalanced and quite antagonistic and angry with everyone. He even kicked his widowed mother out of his home to fend for herself. I never found out whether he overcame his reactions and returned to normal.

Most of us are unaware of the karmic patterns stored within our glands. The Spirit within *does* know. It is far better and safer to let the God within control our spiritual cleansing and development. This is one big reason that Chapter 7 of *A Search For God, Book I* is on the subject of patience. As Hugh Lynn said, ten to fifteen minutes of Silence each time you meditate is sufficient for your cleansing and growth. If you want to meditate three times a day, it is fine but restrict the silent time to that mentioned. Later, as you gain experience in the practice of meditation, you can extend the silent time. Spirit will guide you.

Fourteen Effects of the Movement of the Energy

There are fourteen *basic* effects one might experience while in the Silence. There are many more, but the following are the most commonly encountered in my own meditations and those of dozens of others I have talked with over a period of more than thirty years. I want to make the important point, as stated earlier, that we are *not* seeking visions and experiences of any kind while in the Silence. There will be some involuntary ones, of course. The main ones are outlined here.

1. Head Drawn Backward
You may feel your head tilting backward as if unseen hands are doing the pulling. Go with the flow; it is simply one of the manifestations of the movement of En-

ergy. You can resist the backward movement if you choose, but it's better to just relax and let it happen. Your head may return to upright on its own, or you may choose to bring it back to vertical. If so, it may move to the rear again. Let it happen. From the readings:

(A) The nearer the body of an individual ... draws to the attunement, or consciousness ... as is *in* the Christ Consciousness, the nearer does the body ... become a channel for *Life—living* life—to others to whom the thought is directed. Hence at such periods, these are the manifestations of the life, or the spirit, acting *through* the body. 281-5

2. Coolness of the Forehead

While in the Silence, you might have the sensation of cool air blowing on you, despite the fact that there is no source, such as a fan, to cause the feeling. According to the readings, when this sensation occurs, often a spirit guide or angel is breathing upon you. This was the experience I had when attempting meditation on my own for the very first time. At the time, I wondered what was happening. The room was warm, and no air was stirring. I discovered the reason only after digging into the readings on meditation, such as the following:

(A) As would be termed—literal—as the breath of an angel, or the breath of a master. As the body attunes self ... it may be a channel where there may be even *instant* healing with the laying on of hands. 281-5

3. Loss of Hands and/or Feet

By this, I mean losing awareness of them. It is such a real sensation that you may even open your eyes to see if they are still there, or you may wiggle your fingers or toes for verification. After you return to stilling the mind, you may lose track of them again. This sensation is common with meditators.

4. Body Movements

There are three distinct types of body movements that may occur during meditation, according to Cayce (see 281-12). They are the body swaying gently forward and backward, swaying from side to side, and, swaying in a circular motion. The sensation is real enough that meditators often open their eyes to check themselves, only to find they are not moving at all. The internal movement of Energy causes the sensation. When you close your eyes again, usually the swaying sensation will return. It is rare to discover the physical body moving, though I have occasionally seen veteran meditators have actual body movements. However, such body movements do not necessarily indicate an advanced meditator. I had a lot of body swaying in the early years of my meditating—more than twenty-five years ago—but have had none since. I consider myself an advanced meditator. It is no longer important for me to experience "effects."

5. Extension of the Body

While in the Silence, you may have the distinct feeling that your upper body is extended upward and almost touches the ceiling. This feeling, also, is very realistic, and you will likely open your eyes. When you close your eyes and return to the Silence, the extended feeling often returns. Again, you open your eyes to discover nothing has changed with your body. There is no explanation as to why this anomaly occurs, but it is another manifestation of the movement of Energy through the body during the Silence.

6. Palms Sweaty or Excessively Warm

This is one of the most common reactions to Energy movement. As we stated earlier, excessive warmth or heat is common during the Silence. It is even more obvious during the healing time following the Silence when, if in a group meditation, all the participants join hands to increase the power of the healing vibrations sent out. Such an effect is akin to connecting a series of batteries to gain a stronger power supply.

7. Excessive Heat

Perhaps this is the most common indication of Energy expression. Heat affects the whole body, and the meditator may feel the air conditioning has been shut off or the central heating turned up. On more than one occasion, we have experimented with a thermometer during a group meditation with fifteen or more people involved and discovered an increase of from one to two degrees in the thermometer reading.

8. Dizziness, Lightness in the Head

This is self-explanatory. Some have described this sensation as a "fullness" in the head. I, personally, have most often experienced a dizziness or lightness in my head. The readings indicate a healing Energy here:

> . . . as an active force emanating from the Life itself within. Then, these become all-embracing; hence the better understanding should be gained, whether used to disseminate and bring healing or for the raising of the forces in self. When one is able to so raise within themselves such vibrations, . . . then the body of that individual becomes a magnet that may (if properly used) bring healing to others with the laying on of hands. 281-14

9. Feeling of Energy Moving Up/Down the Spine
I would describe this sensation as a little mouse running up and down my spine, sometimes ending up as a feeling of a fullness in the head as mentioned in Number 8 above.

10. Loss of Consciousness (but not as in falling asleep)
This is one of the most interesting manifestations of all. It is difficult to put into words. We often go to sleep during the Silence because we are so relaxed. When we awaken, we realize we have fallen asleep. But I am referring to a period of unconsciousness different from the sleep state. When you return to the conscious state, you know you have been unconscious rather than asleep, but you don't know where, if anywhere, you may have been. I can only say you will know the distinction between the two when you have the experience. I have never been able to bring back to my memory any awareness where I have been or what I may have been doing during this time. It would be most intriguing to know. It is frequently related to time-distortion as discussed in Number 14. (A detailed explanation of this is given on page 49.)

11. Tingling of Body Parts
At times, various parts of the body might tingle, like the feeling of pins and needles in an arm or leg that has gone to sleep from restricted blood circulation. This can occur in hands, feet, fingers, toes, ear lobes, the tip of the nose, etc., and, again, simply indicates the movement of Energy.

12. Pulsating Lights
While your eyes are closed, you may see soft, opaque, pulsating lights. They usually alternate between one eye and the other. Colors may be seen. (I nearly always see a deep blue or purple.)

13. Sensations in the Eyes

For me, this is a feeling of pressure on the eyeballs themselves. It indicates a personal healing is occurring:

(Q) [295] What is the cause of the sensation I feel in my eyes at times during meditation?

(A) As is manifest by the activities of those that would bring healing to others, the healing of every sort must come first in self that it may be raised in another. This is the healing in self, with that raising of the vision that may heal in others. 281-12

14. Time Distortion

This is the most startling and provocative experience of them all! It is nearly always connected to the type of loss of consciousness listed under Number 10. It is always a good idea to look at the clock when entering your meditation so you will be aware of the time distortion when it occurs. I always check my watch upon entering and completing my meditations.

Here are two of my own experiences. I started my meditation one evening at 11:00 p.m. sharp. After the meditation, I had the clear feeling it was an unusually long one. I looked at my watch: 11:05 p.m. I could not believe it. I thought my watch had stopped. I checked other clocks in the house; they all had the same time of 11:05 p.m. The reason this experience was strange to me is that my normal daily meditations follow a pattern of relaxation, prayer, the Silence, the healing prayer and the thanksgiving prayer, which invariably takes twenty-five to thirty-five minutes, but during this time distortion meditation, I went through all the phases in only five minutes.

At the opposite end of the spectrum of time distortion, on another occasion, I started my evening meditation at 11:00 p.m. It seemed to last only a short time. When I checked my watch, I was shocked to see it was 4:15 a.m.

I had been in meditation more than five hours. I had not only lost consciousness, but lost track of time as well.

The most interesting time distortion I ever encountered involved a large group. I was a primary speaker for an A.R.E. weekend retreat held at Mo-Ranch outside of Kerrville, Texas, during the early 1970s. The theme was meditation. It was customary for our retreats to end with a special healing meditation that usually lasted an hour or more, depending on the number of participants. I was to lead the meditation and noticed we were running late. The time was 11:40 a.m. and lunch was scheduled for noon. Since twenty minutes wasn't enough for the healing meditation, I asked the camp personnel to delay lunch until 12:30 p.m., to which they graciously consented. We began our healing meditation at 11:45 a.m. and followed the usual meditation steps of relaxation, opening prayer time, the Silence of five to ten minutes (I thought), and the normal healing prayer time until we reached the period for the special "laying on of hands." We had about seven "channels" acting as laying-on-of-hands healers standing behind seven chairs set up for this occasion. Every one of the forty-five attendees present came forward for a healing, which generally required fifteen or twenty minutes. When we completed the healing and ended with a prayer of thanksgiving, the time was straight up noon! Under normal circumstances, it would be impossible to conduct such a meditation in fifteen minutes. We reveled in the knowledge that we collectively had experienced a genuine time distortion. I have never since been exposed to such a group time distortion, but it is one I shall never forget.

Experiences one can have during the Silence are by no means limited to the fourteen reported here. I have discussed with my seminar attendees many, many more that are unique to the individuals involved. The ones discussed here are only the most frequently encountered.

7

Fruits of the Spirit

T here are many fringe benefits from daily meditation. Although I would be the first to say these benefits should not be our primary reason for learning to meditate, I want to list some of the fruits of the Spirit generated by our efforts.

Perhaps it would be helpful here to explain my use of the phrase "fruits of the Spirit." I recognize that many readers will think the phrase refers to those fruits of the Spirit listed by the apostle Paul in his letter to the Galatians:

> But the fruit of the spirit is love, joy, peace, longsuffering, gentleness, goodness, faith, meekness, temperance: Galatians 5:22

I am using the phrase in a broader sense: When we meditate daily, the Spirit of God within us begins to come forth more openly and actively in many, many areas of our life-expression—the physical and mental, as well as the spiritual—including the all-important *balance* among these different aspects of our being.

Although I want to discuss here the benefits of meditation, there are some events and situations in our lives that might be interpreted as negative. We shall see, however, that these are positive, soul-growth experiences that only *appear* to be negative. (We will look at some of these a little later in the book.) For now, I will share with you the obviously *positive* fruits that come to us. I am quite sure there are many more beneficial effects than listed here. They are limited, naturally, to the experience, needs, and consciousness of the meditator. They are presented in no order of importance. This, too, varies among individuals:

1. A Heightened Sensitivity/An Expanded Consciousness

One or more, and possibly all five, of the physical senses become more acute. For example, there are times when my sense of smell seems to be more acute, or the sense of feeling, as when I have occasionally experienced a gentle breeze as extremely energetic. This quickening can also be felt in the mental, emotional, or intuitive parts of us. It may be expressed through psychic receptiveness, such as clairvoyance (seeing), clairaudience (hearing), or clairsentience (feeling). My own psychic sensitivity has manifested itself through my considerably increased clairsentience.

2. Sharper Memory and Recall/Better Problem Solving

Better memory and recall seem to occur only when I am in need of them, rather than as a constant state. I have better, clearer dream recall when I need it for guidance or when I'm trying to solve a problem.

3. Better Sleep and Relaxation

I find I can sleep just about anywhere—even aboard planes and trains, for instance, and usually under the most distracting conditions, depending upon my needs.

4. Better Physiological Control

On more than one occasion, I have been able to affect a physical problem in my body. For example, before my meditation days, if I turned my ankle, it would become swollen and quite painful. Since learning to tap meditation Energy, on two such occasions, I was able to sit down immediately after the incident, put my hand on the affected ankle, and treat it with my mind by directing the pain to go away, and no swelling to ensue. As a result, the swelling was minimal, and the pain was relieved within a few minutes.

Common sense is called for here. A recurring or persistent pain is, of course, a message from the body that something is wrong. Persistent pain should be checked by a qualified healing practitioner, whether medical or holistic. The mind possesses great healing powers, although few of us are properly trained and disciplined enough to control these powers.

5. Better Balance in One's Life

One of Cayce's major themes is the individual's need to achieve balance among the physical, mental, and spiritual aspects of his being. These aspects represent the three-dimensional expression of the soul while it resides in the earth plane. Most of us are aware of the *ex-*

treme expression of any of these three natures of our being: the earth-earthy materialist indulging in the excesses of the body—sex, food, drugs, etc.; the intellectual who gives importance to knowledge above all else; the spiritual or religious fanatic with tunnel vision for his own belief system. Meditation has a decided effect in helping balance the individual away from extremes; thus, meditators become more sensitive to any extremism they are expressing in one of these areas. We begin to seek outwardly the balance we intrinsically know and desire to achieve. The more effort applied in this direction, the more help we receive from meditation. Remember, we choose to cooperate with the God within. The Spirit within, seeing we mean business, begins to guide us in achieving the balance we seek. A three-legged stool will only be useful if all three legs are the same length.

6. More Energy/Strength

The flow of Energy is one of the earliest and easiest effects to recognize while meditating. It is also one of the foremost manifestations in our conscious daily lives. We begin to realize that our batteries have been fully recharged. We don't become depleted of energy quite as much, nor as frequently, as we once did, even though we are getting physically older with each passing day. When a situation arises requiring some extra energy or strength, we find it is there.

There are many stories related to Energy from my own experiences over the years, but I will recount only one to make my point.

A few years ago, I was giving many weekend seminars for the A.R.E. During this time, I was also deeply involved in ballroom dancing. I had been taking both private and group lessons, spending a great deal of my extra time at it. On one occasion, I was scheduled to be in Houston, Texas, at 8:00 a.m. on Saturday to present an all-day seminar on prophecy from 9:00 a.m. to 5:00 p.m. I also had a rare opportunity that week, an invitation for dinner and dancing with an elite group of dancers on Friday evening before the Saturday seminar. The party was to be held in a private club with an orchestra. The arrangements would allow the ten couples involved to enjoy a spacious dance floor—a dancer's delight and a rarity. This was an invitation I could not turn down.

I lived at the time in Dallas, a little more than a four-hour drive from Houston. The party was to end by 1:00 a.m., which would give me time enough to drive to Houston for the seminar. I arrived in Houston at 5:30 in the morning, checked into the motel where the seminar was to be conducted and got an hour and a half's sleep. After a hearty breakfast, I gave what I felt was one of my better seminars. Other staff members, who knew of my night's driving schedule, wondered where I had gotten my energy, as I was just as energetic at the end of the program as I had been that morning. Of course, my answer was, from the Spirit within. (Also, every speaker receives a tremendous amount of feedback Energy from his audience. I was fortunate to be able to receive a great deal of Energy from the 135 persons in attendance.)

I have had many similar experiences over my more than thirty years of meditation. The Energy required is always there when needed.

7. More Tolerance with Self and Others

Tolerance is a virtue encompassing many attributes: patience, freedom from bigotry, lack of prejudice, a liberal spirit, open-mindedness, receptivity, mercy, benevolence, good will, kindliness, forbearance, acceptance, empathy, and brotherly love. It is an ingredient that, if mixed into and developed in enough of us, would bring on the millennium in peace to the world. It is clearly one definite attribute coming to those who meditate, and the more regular the meditation, the more the tolerance develops.

Prior to my meditation days, I was not a very tolerant person—though had you made such a statement to me at the time, I am sure I would have disagreed with you. Even though I had patience in some areas of my life, there were too many in which I had none. I most certainly was not free of bigotry and prejudice, and although I was a fairly liberal spirit, I was not as open-minded and receptive to others' thinking, opinions, and ways of expressing life as I would want others to be with me. I had neither the tolerance nor the empathy to understand or accept others as they were. You might say that, at times, I was self-righteous, thought I knew best, and would judge another's character without the tolerance required to express brotherly love.

There is not space here to list the many ways I failed to show tolerance, but let me give one good example. After I found the loving wisdom of the Cayce readings and joined the A.R.E., I became quite intolerant and judgmental of the orthodox Christian group to which I had previously belonged. I thought they were stupid and closed-minded to make judgments about the Cayce readings, such as charging that Cayce was used and controlled by the devil. This infuriated me, and, of course, I was being just as judgmental as I was accusing *them* of being. After a few years of daily meditation, my attitude began to change, slowly at first, then more rapidly.

I have had many opportunities to practice tolerance since that time, but one set of circumstances stands out in particular. For the last few years, since I lost my "permanent" rent location because the landlord's wife desired it for one of her female friends, I have had the challenge of living with several different landlords (most of whom were personal friends of mine). In each case, the landlord owned the home and I rented a bedroom, with kitchen and house privileges.

It has always been a part of my philosophy to practice, to the best of my ability, the first lesson given in *A Search for God, Book I*—Cooperation—especially when living with another person under the same roof. Over a period of three years, I found it necessary to move and spend rental time with four different persons. All were past fifty, had been living alone for a long time, and were quite set in their ways. It was my policy to live with them according to their house rules. I soon discovered that much tolerance, patience, and understanding were required of me in each case if peace was to be maintained. Let me simply say that I was stretched to improve my tolerance level, which, of course, is the way we learn and develop any soul attribute—by having to exercise and use it in our daily lives. Meditation habitually gives us a virtue that life will then give us opportunities to apply. That is how we grow.

8. Guidance/An Inner Knowing/Calmness

On more than one occasion, I have had people ask, "What is it you have that I want?" They sense a relaxed calmness and serenity radiating from the Spirit within, certainly with no credit toward anything I have done with my life other than to meditate regularly. I recall a time my landlord informed me someone had broken into my car, but it did not upset me at all. In fact, my first thought was one of thankfulness that it had not been stolen and stripped, never to be seen again. It was a little inconvenient, as I had to have it towed to the repair shop to replace the broken window and the steering wheel damaged during the attempt to hot-wire the ignition. At least I still had a car. Before my meditation days, I would have been very angry and full of resentment toward the perpetrators of such an act.

9. A Conscious Awareness of the Silence

This does not occur often, but when it does, it is spiritual ecstasy. I frequently refer to this unusual manifestation as "the thunder of the Silence." Such a statement may appear to be a contradiction or an oxymoron, as alluded to earlier when I discussed how loud the Silence can sometimes be. When I say a conscious hearing of the Silence, I mean just that. Sometimes I am walking down a busy street with people bustling, horns honking, and various other noises occurring in our everyday world, or I may be in a busy airport, waiting for an arriving flight amid all the noise associated with such a place. In both of these situations, I have experienced the Silence. It was so loud I could not help but hear and be aware of it. However, it was not disturbing or distracting. I simply became aware of the Silence in the midst of outward physical activities. It usually lasted only a minute or two, but was quite profound when it happened, making an indelible impression. I liken it to being a direct gift from the Father-Mother God to remind us that Spirit is with us all the time. I once had a doctor try to tell me I was just experiencing tinnitus (a ringing in the ears). I told him that I have experienced tinnitus and know the difference.

10. A New Attitude/Empathy Toward Life

The empathy effect is closely associated with the increased tolerance discussed in Number 7. We experience ourselves embracing a whole new attitude toward life and all the people with whom we are thrown together. We become less judgmental of others and their shortcomings. We begin to see situations and problems from an entirely new perspective, one allowing more objectivity than ever before. Empathy means the ability to project ourselves into another person's situation and viewpoint, thus giving us greater objectivity. This new 360-degree vision makes life much easier to deal with.

We no longer get very upset at the idiosyncrasies of others; we no longer permit ourselves to fall into emotional turmoil at the unfairness we see around us.

I am reminded of the story of the doctor whose female patient was a habitual complainer with a very negative view of life. He suggested she begin to think more positively, to find the bright side in every situation, and to meditate on the love of God and the inherent goodness in people. He asked her to return and report to him in a month. When she returned, he asked her how things were in her life and whether she had changed her attitude. She replied, "No, I haven't changed, but I do notice other people are much nicer." Before beginning to meditate, we often refuse to admit anything is wrong with ourselves.

11. A Greater, More Positive Self-Image

Although this benefit is a result of all of the others, we discover how unique and wonderful we really are. We begin to love ourselves as we are loved. We begin to see ourselves as God sees us. We realize we are no greater but also no lesser than any other soul in the earth, regardless of rank, position, or wealth. This realization is worth its weight in gold and transforms us into the people we have always wanted to be. It aids us in stopping the foolish and fruitless act of comparing ourselves to others and their accomplishments. We begin to realize that each soul enters the earth plane with a specific, self-chosen destiny. Some of us will become little cogs in the wheel of life, quietly and joyfully fulfilling the purpose we entered to accomplish, whether we are rich or poor, famous or unknown. The Cayce readings inform us that the soul is always aware of its destiny, regardless of our *conscious* awareness of that destiny.

A positive self-image helps us to be at peace with ourselves. It also helps us to be more joyful in our lifestyle which, in turn, attracts new friends. People are attracted to happy, joyful people and like to be around them, as their vibrations are much more positive—even though they may not be consciously aware of the attraction.

I consider these eleven attributes of meditation to be the *minor* fruits of the Spirit. I will discuss the major ones later in this chapter. There are many more minor attributes that I could list. They are, as mentioned earlier, limited only to the individual meditator.

I alluded to my "Joshua experience" earlier. I have already shared with you a great deal of the story in Chapter 4, when I discussed the trauma I encountered when my wife divorced me in the early 1970s, during the time my business also failed and I went heavily in debt.

Although I did not know it at the time, I was entering into the most spiritually uplifting period of soul growth in my life, even though my whole "playhouse" was torn down during these events. Now I can see the wisdom and value of not being able to know the future. Had I known what I was destined to experience, I am quite sure I would have taken a different path and run the other way. Of course, running away would have deprived me of my greatest lesson-learning opportunity of this lifetime (at least up to this point in my life).

In Chapter 4, I shared with you many of the negative things which happened to me during this five-year period of being mostly unemployed. Now, I'll tell you about some of the positive episodes connected with this experience.

First, and most important, the years spent in daily meditation paid off quite beneficially. I remained calm and peaceful nearly all of the time. I had the most prolific dream recall and guidance I have ever experienced. Not only did I receive several guiding and educational dreams, I also was able to accurately interpret them almost instantly upon awakening (something at which I had never been so adept before). Literally, all of my basic needs were met in the way of housing, transportation, food, and enough money to meet the demands of the day. I had the opportunity to live in the country with the quietness of nature all around me, which was most healing to the spirit, mind, and body. I had a deep and abiding love relationship, which helped to heal me and which has become, to this day, a special and durable friendship. I learned how little one needs to survive comfortably in this materially oriented society.

Earlier, I related that my teenage son had come to live with me and was involved with drugs. Many years later, when he was drug-free and we were reminiscing, he told me that he had thought during his teens that I was a drug pusher. I asked him why he thought this, and he replied, "I noticed you always had enough money to see us through. I knew only drug pushers had that kind of money." I nearly broke up with laughter.

All of this brings me to the explanation of my "Joshua experience." Before I relate it, let me clarify what I mean by that phrase. Actually, I should call this experience "my *almost* Joshua experience." As you read the Joshua story, you will see how the Israelites lost their faith during their forty-year sojourn in the desert. In my case, I kept my faith because I had the meditation Energy received during my early years of meditation. In fact the Energy gave me the faith, assurance, strength, and guidance I needed to get through such a "hard-times" episode. Rather, the whole five-year encounter increased my faith to a much greater magnitude. Some would liken such an experience to a "dark night of the soul," as it is often called by the religious community.

In Unity's *Metaphysical Bible Dictionary*, there is a great and wonderful story about Joshua. (This very enlightening and revealing book, published by The Unity School of Christianity, Unity Village, MO 64065, interprets the many patriarchs, persons, and places mentioned in the Bible.):

> Joshua was Moses' right-hand man and the leader of Moses' army. He was one of two spies who gave a good report on the Promised Land. He took charge of the Israelites after the death of Moses and led them into the land of Canaan.

Let me share with you my interpretation and understanding of that story. Although it was *my* "Joshua experience," I think it is an experience that happens to many, if not all, spiritual seekers on the path as part of their spiritual growth.

> Metaphysically, *Joshua* means "Jah is savior, Jehovah is deliverer." In the Hebrew the name is identical with the name Jesus.

A most interesting point, since the Cayce readings give Joshua as one of the past lives of Jesus.

> Both of these names are derived from the word *Jehovah,* meaning "I AM THAT I AM." The only difference between the names Joshua and Jesus is the extent of conscious realization of identity with the I AM. In certain states of mind, the I AM in man acquires greatly increased power.

Meditation, with the right ideal, can give that increased power.

> Joshua took the Children of Israel into the Promised Land (spiritual realization). So it is through the power of our I AM, or indwelling Christ, that we lay hold of and attain the redemption of our life forces.

When Moses died and Joshua took command, he notified the Children of Israel that they would pass over into the Promised Land in three days. This promptness of action is the result of confidence and power.

Refer to the minor fruits of the Spirit, numbers 6, 8, and 11, given in this chapter. We learn and gain this type of power through our daily meditations, giving us the energy and courage to take whatever action life requires of us to direct our own destiny.

Joshua was the spiritual leader of his people. As long as they kept their spiritual connection with him, they were doubly fruitful, but when they turned away from his leadership, they fell back into materiality.

The death of Joshua and the falling away of the Children of Israel into idolatry after he died can be explained metaphysically this way: *As night follows the day, so, in the early religious experiences of the soul, a season of darkness always follows a high illumination.* At this time, the untried powers of the soul and its past sins and shortcomings are brought into evidence; apparently, disorder and confusion prevail. But in the light of Truth, this experience is not a going back. *It is only a letting go in order to get a better hold.* The unalterable laws of God are constantly working to bring into expression the poise and serenity and joy of Divine Mind, or the I AM within.[1] (Emphasis added.)

When I began my Joshua experience, I had been meditating more than ten years. There were times, during the

---

[1] *Metaphysical Bible Dictionary*, Unity School of Christianity, p. 369. Used with permission.

first couple of years of that five-year "experience," when I felt I was going backwards. Upon reflection, I certainly could find places, actions, and events in the prior ten years of meditating during which I may well have misused my newfound powers and awareness. I was not sure. When I first read the Joshua story, I really wondered whether I had lost the greater Light. Certainly, I had experienced some high illumination via my meditations. It also certainly appeared I had fallen back into the darkness, with all that had happened to me. However, as I studied and meditated upon the Joshua story more and more, I soon realized I was letting go to get a better hold, as the story stated:

> . . . The final step into light out of this season of darkness is the dawning of a new day. When all human means of deliverance have failed, the only source of escape is to turn within to the one Helper. When Spirit is appealed to, the freeing power is set into activity and the path that leads into the light is made clear . . . though one may go down into the depths temporarily, the beacon light of spiritual illumination is not extinguished; those who have learned to trust the Lord, to keep their faces turned toward the light *[through meditation]* regardless of appearances, are learning to pass from one state of consciousness to another . . . with little or no disturbance. They have learned to make practical use of divine law; to walk unafraid on the waters of untried seas of thought.[2]

I repeat, my Joshua experience was the greatest spiritual growth period of my life. And it was the daily medi-

---

[2]Ibid., page 369f.

tation energy and the guidance I received during this time that gave me the strength and the direction to get through it.

As given earlier, the eleven attributes of the Spirit described previously are what I call the *minor fruits* of the Spirit. There are major ones also, which I consider to have a far more important and powerful effect on our soul growth. They relate more to our spiritual nature and how it guides us more and more into the realm of service to others.

As our consciousness is raised by our meditation, so are many new opportunities for soul-growth afforded us. Our soul evolution is speeded up in a manner that seems to make our lives more hectic at times. It is because, as we grow spiritually, our soul's responsibilities increase. The more we know and learn, the more is expected of us. I recall in my very early A.R.E. days how I was perturbed over a Cayce reading that issued a warning about studying the material in the readings. In effect, it warned seekers not to study the material unless they had every intention of putting what they learned into practice in their everyday lives. We would be far better off to turn away from the readings and forget them than to learn what is expected of us for our soul growth and then fail to apply it. In essence, we would create more karma for ourselves by sins of omission, after learning what to do, than if we just walked away from them and remained ignorant. This frightened me a bit because I was not sure I was up to applying the spiritual principles the readings discussed. Like most seekers, however, my desire for a better and more productive life won out over my fears.

Perhaps another analogy would be apropos here to clarify the "hectic times" mentioned in the previous paragraph. It is one I have used many times in my seminars to explain the "ups and downs" of soul growth when one becomes a daily meditator. When a person decides to initiate the practice and discipline of daily meditation certain changes in lifestyle and soul growth begin to appear in their life after a certain amount of time—this time varying according to their "soul status" or level of consciousness at the time of incorporating daily meditation into their life. For the first few months, or more likely a year or two, the meditator's life seems to smooth out and they begin to enjoy fewer problems and more control over their lives. Then, when everything seems to be going serenely and calmly, all hell seems to break loose, and they find themselves embroiled in a whole new set of circumstances and "lesson-learning" experiences. This is because they have mastered the lessons given to them on their current level of awareness or consciousness and have graduated to a new level, akin to graduating from high school as a senior where they were experienced, respected, and in control, and a few months later, starting college as a freshman where they are new and uneducated to the requirements of college and are considered to be just "frosh" who are young, stupid, and inexperienced.

I consider the qualities listed below to be the major fruits of the Spirit, and, again, they are not given in any order of priority. To me, they are all important to soul growth:

1. Enhanced Prayer Activity

Perhaps a better way of putting it is to say meditation improves and increases our personal contact with God. We are more alert to who we really are: Each of us is a spiritual being who is a part of the Godhead and knows itself to be itself and yet one with the Father-Mother God Principle:

> That it, the entity, may *know* itself to *be* itself and part of the Whole; not the Whole but one *with* the

whole; and thus retaining its individuality, knowing itself to be itself yet one with the purposes of the First Cause that called it, the entity, into *being*, into the awareness, into the consciousness of itself. 826-11

This realization will not lead us to become religious or spiritual fanatics unless we permit ourselves to get out of balance. We are simply more aware of our Higher Selves and, therefore, talk with the God within more often than in the past.

2. Strengthened Will Power

Meditation vastly improves our daily choices, the way and direction in which we use our will. As I tell all my seminar students: In reality, we only need to make one choice. We simply need to choose to meditate every day. Meditation alone, by the mere force and power of the Energy contacted, will make all our other daily choices better ones. We will find ourselves automatically refusing those activities that might interfere with soul growth and embracing those that will enhance it.

3. Help in Manifesting the Fruits of the Spirit of the Christ

Those fruits are patience, compassion, kindness, long-suffering, persistence, virtue, understanding, empathy, and love for all persons (including yourself) and all living creatures.

The word *long-suffering* is interpreted by too many to denote only pain. If you look up the word *suffer* in the dictionary, you will find that, in addition to feeling hurt and pain, it means to *permit* or *allow*, as in Jesus' statement, "Suffer the little children to come unto me . . . " (Mark 10:14) and to *experience*, to *perceive*, to *learn*. Thus, through long-suffering, we are learning and allowing wisdom to come into our lives by what we experience and by that to which we are exposed.

Let's compare the above with what the apostle Paul and Edgar Cayce had to say about the fruits of the spirit. In the King James version, Paul said, "But the fruit of the Spirit is love, joy, peace, long-suffering*, gentleness*, goodness, faith, meekness*, temperance*: against such there is no law." (Gal. 5:22-23) The Revised Standard version is slightly different: "But the fruit of the Spirit is love, joy, peace, patience*, kindness*, goodness, faithfulness, gentleness*, self-control*; against such there is no law." The asterisked words replace each other according to the biblical interpreter.

A couple of Edgar Cayce readings give the following:

> . . . the comparisons that make for Life itself in its *essence,* as for harmony, peace, joy, love, long-suffering, patience, brotherly love, kindness—these are the fruits of the Spirit. 5754-2

> . . . in the consciousness of all the fruits of the spirit: fellowship, kindness, gentleness, patience, long-suffering, love; these be the fruits of the spirit. Against such there is no law. 5752-3

I would like to give my personal understanding and interpretation of the word *meekness,* since the word was used in the King James version of Paul's "fruits of the Spirit". If you look the word up in Rodale's *The Synonym Finder,* you will find fifty-one synonyms given for the word *meekness,* all of which may be proper in the context of the user's understanding, use, and definition of the word. In researching the Cayce readings on the subject, I found five very interesting uses of the word:

> . . . that the activity of patience is **meekness** in

action, pureness in heart . . . 262-25

Not that the entity in its **meekness** is not capable of being fired by emotions event even to madness or anger. These are well. For they that are not capable of becoming emotional over their own ideas and ideals are very lax, but those who may not control same are in a sad plight indeed! 1129-2

. . . let not thyself grow angry—with thine own self or with others; but manifest **meekness** humbleness—yes, **meekness;** not in being ashamed, no. 2390-9

. . . that the Son of Man comes—humble, gently, kind, **meek,** lowly—for "He that is the greatest among you serveth all." 3161-1

(Q) How can the body approach her daughter, [5562] without annoying her?
(A) In the **meekness** of truth; not as coddling, not as pitying, but rather in the **strength** of doing that as will enable the . . . daughter to understand the strength that is within self . . . 5563-1) [Author's emphasis in bold.]

Meekness does not imply weakness, as some suppose. Rather, it implies, to me, the spiritual strength within the person to remain in control of one's emotions in order to manifest a peaceful and workable solution to a potentially hostile situation. It takes a great deal more spiritual strength of character to walk away from a fight than to become embroiled in one. The meek are the strong. The third beatitude of Christ's Sermon on the Mount was: "Blessed are the meek, for they shall inherit the earth." (Matthew 5:5)

4. A New Sense of Oneness with God and All Living Things

A new sense of oneness begins to develop, allowing us to see the connection among all living things. We begin to pay closer attention to the birds, the animals, and the insects, and to the parts they play in the scheme of life. In this new feeling of oneness with God, we find ourselves having more understanding, compassion, and empathy with all peoples, especially those toward whom we may have felt some enmity in the past. We find it easier to forgive and overlook another person's faults and shortcomings. We look at all life from a totally new perspective.

5. Changed Attitudes Toward Life

To sum up the thirty or forty minutes spent in my seminars on the subject of grace in a few short sentences: Some say grace is a gift from God, given to us through the Christ to enhance our lives, in order that we may more fully enjoy the fruits of the spirit. I agree with that definition of grace as, from my point of view, all things material and immaterial come from the Father and are considered to be His gifts. Others say grace has to be earned by the soul. Perhaps grace lies somewhere in between those two views.

Grace, when you fully analyze it and study what the Cayce readings have to say about it, is really just an *attitude*. The Law of Grace was established in the earth and offered to us by the Christ Spirit, manifested through Jesus and the pattern he gave us in and for the earth. It is available to all; we just need to invoke it by our choices of the attitudes we take toward our fellow humans, their actions, and whatever conditions or events prevail in our lives. Another way of saying it is that grace is an energy released into our lives and experienced by us if we adopt attitudes conducive to its "flow." Here are a couple of extracts from the Cayce readings that support my view that grace can be activated in our lives, any time we so desire, by our attitudes toward life:

> For as these conditions are partially karmic, with the correct **attitude,** in grace much may be accomplished. 3177-1

> . . . But the [karmic] law is not taken away—it must be fulfilled every whit, every jot and tittle. Under what law **choosest** *thou* to be aware, or to work? These are the **choices** of men . . . 2650-1

> . . . meeting those things which have been called karmic, yet remembering that **under the law of grace** this may not be **other than an urge . . . may take the choice** that makes for life, love, joy, happiness. 1771-2 [Author's emphasis in bold.]

The reader may ask here, "How can two laws (karma and grace) operate simultaneously?" Let me share with you an analogy I first heard from Hugh Lynn Cayce which answers this question. If you take a bucketful of water and turn it upside down, the law of gravity will cause the water to spill. However, if you take that same bucket and rapidly sling it around and around over your head, the law of centrifugal force is activated, which counteracts the effects of the law of gravity; one balances out the other, but both laws are still operating. Another analogy: If I hold up my left hand and strike the left palm very hard with my right fist, this is pure karma being met full force; however, if I should raise my hand to a higher elevation with my palm facing downward—by choosing to be in a state of grace, or activating the law of grace—rising above the path of the oncoming fist, the fist will still hit my left palm but only in a glancing blow. The state of grace that I am choosing to be in would considerably nullify the effect of the oncoming karma due to my *attitude* of loving indifference and acceptance. The karma is still being met, but in the higher consciousness of the state of grace; the law of grace is softening and somewhat diffusing the law of karma. By our daily choices, we control and exhibit our attitudes and reactions to any given person or situation. We project ourselves into a state of grace, or we do not, depending on those choices we make at any given time and circumstance. Here are two incidents which offer good examples of how one's attitude can activate the Law of Grace:

Two friends go away for the weekend on a fishing trip and return home to find their adjacent homes completely cleaned out by burglars. The first man becomes very angry and upset, vowing to track them down and exact every ounce of retribution he can. The second is just thankful no one in his family was harmed—he knows he can eventually replace the stolen articles. He knows there is not much he can do except report the incident to the police and hope to get some of the articles returned. He accepts what has happened to him and determines he will not let it ruin his life. He clearly is in a state of grace. As I say, grace is an attitude. We can slip into or out of it at our choosing. And meditation makes the choice of grace easier for us to employ in our lives.

The second is a delightful story of two Hindu sages (from Alan Watts' Introduction to *Spiritual Practices of India*) that is a perfect analogy of how an attitude can project one into a state of Grace:

Two sages were meditating in the forest in order to realize the union of their inmost selves with God. One had sat, without moving, in the lotus position for over seven years—so still that moss had grown up around him, covering his shoulders and upper torso. Birds nested in his hair, and snakes crawled unnoticed over his legs. The second sage danced merrily around a tree, singing his praises to the Lord Brahma. The Hindus think of God in three aspects: Brahma the creator, Vishnu the preserver, and Shiva the destroyer.

Now one day, Vishnu came down to earth in the guise of his human form, Krishna. Krishna walked through the forest where the two sages were meditating. When Krishna came upon the first sage, the sage was startled out of his profound concentration in the presence of this divine being. On seeing Krishna before him, the sage was so eager to ask about the problem which had so long occupied his mind that he hardly took the time to make the proper reverences. "Oh, Krishna," he blurted out, "when you return to heaven, will you please ask the Supreme Brahma how long it will take me to attain union with Him and final release from the human state?" To this Krishna agreed and, continuing his journey, likewise consented to the same request from the second sage who was dancing merrily around the tree.

The following day, Krishna returned from heaven. He again took his walk through the forest. "Have you been back to heaven?" cried the first sage. "And did you ask the Supreme Brahma how long I must yet meditate before attaining the highest Realization?"

"Indeed, I did," replied Krishna, "and I have good news for you. His message is that you will attain after being born again into the earth only three more times."

"Yet three more times!" wailed the sage, in utter disappointment. "Do you mean that these many, many years and many incarnations I have struggled to control my mind, to plumb the depths of my soul, sitting here like a rock through heat and cold, sun and rain, subduing my passions, denying myself the pleasures of life and concentrating all the powers of my being have been in vain? Do you mean I must still toil and sacrifice through three more lives?" At this, Krishna passed on, leaving the first sage in a state of black despair.

"Ah, Krishna!!" sang the second sage at the approach of the god. "You must have come back from heaven already. Did you see the Supreme Brahma and ask Him how long it must be before I can attain the Great Release and know I am one with Him?"

"Oh yes," answered Krishna, a shade reluctantly. "Yes, I did."

"And what did He have to say?" asked the sage.

"My friend," said Krishna, "the Supreme Brahma told me that you must work on and still be born into the world as many times as there are leaves upon this tree about which you dance."

The sage gazed into the tree. "Indeed," he mused, "there cannot be many more than ten thousand leaves up there." And then he cried out, "Oh Krishna, you mean I have only ten thousand more lives to live in the earth! Only ten thousand? Ah, how can I thank you for these happy, happy tidings!"

At this instant, there came a great Voice from heaven, saying, "My son, in this very moment . . . you have attained!"[3]

The second sage's attitude immediately projected him into a state of grace and the attainment he so joyfully and happily sought.

---

[3] *Spiritual Practices of India*, by Frederic Spiegelberg. San Francisco, The Greenwood Press, 1952. Paraphrased with permission.

6. Becoming a More Powerful, Useful Channel

By opening ourselves up to the Creative Energies of a higher power, the Energy cleanses and prepares you for more and more service to others. For, indeed, we *are* our brother's keeper. Our new capacities will present to us new opportunities to serve others, allowing much of our negative karma to be neutralized or lessened. Indeed, the Cayce readings state that the giving of one's life for another can erase a great deal of negative karma.

8

Working with the Light

When I speak of working with the Light, I mean working and cooperating with the Energy gained from our daily meditations. Light is a synonym for God. The Cayce readings, in fact, give a number of synonyms for God: Law, Truth, Energy, Spirit, Light, Love. From a metaphysical viewpoint, all of these words represent the Creative Energy we call God. How many near-death experiences (NDEs) have you read about in which the person described the fantastic and unusual Light he or she felt, saw, and experienced during the NDE? Chances are, virtually every one did. If you have not read about NDEs,

I suggest two of many good books on the subject: *Embraced by the Light*, by Betty J. Eadie, published by Gold Leaf Press, and *Saved by the Light*, by Dannion Brinkley, published by Random House. Both of these books are inspirational, educational, and well written. I have personally met and talked with Dannion Brinkley and heard several of his lectures. He is a most enlightening and humorous speaker.

I have said we get good, reliable guidance from our daily meditations because of the Energy coming forth in a more powerful, directed way in our lives. I also have said this Energy will guide (if not push) us into various opportunities for service to others.

For example, here is the story of Mark, one of the boys we took in during our first year as foster parents (This account was first published in the November/December 1987 issue of *Venture Inward* magazine, a publication of the A.R.E.):

HE CAME TO US TO DIE

The wind whipped at my heels as I proudly held open the back door to admit Mark, our newest foster son. It was a cool autumn day, but the sun was bright, matching our mood. Certainly that beautiful day in 1967 gave no warning of the soul-searching events to come for Doris and me or her mother, Margie, and the five other foster sons who were to share our home. Nor were we aware, at the time, that Mark would be the focal point of these traumatic events.

Doris and I had been wondering what to do with the eight-bedroom, seven-bathroom home we had bought the year before. It was much too large for just the two of us, and we both believed in using things to their fullest potential. We had felt strongly moved to buy this particular house; indeed, the circumstances of the sale practically thrust it upon us.

Having been active in A.R.E. work for years, we believed strongly in inner guidance and letting the Spirit within direct us toward our best abilities. We were aware of the Energy, guidance, and power available through daily meditation. The readings often say to take the first step and the next one will be shown.

When I read an ad in the newspaper seeking foster homes for brain-damaged students who were sent to Plano Academy in Dallas from out of state, I knew immediately this was the answer for a constructive use of our home. Although we had no experience with foster care, we eagerly applied, were accepted, and agreed to take four boys. But because the school's need was critical, and we had the space, they asked us to take six.

The boys ranged in age from 12 to 17, and each is a story unto himself. However, this story is about Mark, the third of the six who joined our expanding family. Although Mark was neither better nor worse than the rest of the boys, his story is pungently unique and touching to the soul.

This was Mark's second year at the academy, and we had been warned that he was incorrigible. He had made quite a reputation for himself during his previous year as a hostile, belligerent, and most uncooperative 15-year-old. To be sure, Mark was a paradox. When he gazed at you with those big, beautiful, dark brown eyes and flashed his disarming smile, Mark could be the most charming, gracious, affable person one could hope to meet. The next moment he might fly into a tyrannical mood, his smile turning into a scowl, those loving eyes now emitting an intense, venomous look of hatred.

Born with a cleft palate, Mark had undergone corrective surgery that left him with a faint scar and an ever-so-slight speech impairment. He was also a diabetic and required 40 to 60 units of insulin per day. The condition was discovered when he was five years old. If there was anything in he world he hated, it was those daily insulin shots. Even though Mark had almost died the year before while in a diabetic coma and was aware of the importance of the insulin to the maintenance and safety of his health, he frequently tried to fool me with his daily urinalysis test by putting plain water in the test tube in place of his urine to escape those despised insulin needles.

I am sure both of these conditions contributed to his general animosity toward the world; few people, if any, escaped his wrath at some point.

Mark loved to eat. Unfortunately, he especially loved the foods prohibited by his diabetic condition. It was most difficult for us to control his sugar intake. He sneaked to the refrigerator whenever he could, and he was always buying sweets and hiding them. It was tough to convince him of the danger of his eating habits.

The day after Mark arrived he got into his first fight with one of his foster brothers. By the end of the month, he had fought each of the other five boys at least once. It was a rare day that an altercation involving him did not occur. If no disturbance was in progress, it seemed that Mark was always willing to get something going.

A pivotal point in my relationship with the boys, and Mark in particular, was the one time I really showed any intense anger toward him. He had been living with us four or five weeks. Mark and his 13-year-old roommate, Bob, had been fighting almost constantly since their arrival from school one day. Invariably Mark was the one who started the trouble. I had stopped fights between them at least a half dozen times. Finally, in disgust and despair, I stopped one more fight and ordered Mark to go to his room. I knew the other four boys were upstairs in their rooms so I specifically directed him to go straight to his own room and to talk to no one.

A few minutes later, while I was counseling with Bob, I heard a loud, heavy noise upstairs as though a heavy object had been dropped or thrown. As I arrived at the top of the stairs, Mark was cowering on the floor outside of 16-year-old Wes' room. I looked into the room and saw a large hole in the wall at eye level. Wes explained that Mark came into his room and started an argument. Wes became angry and took a swing at Mark. Fortunately, Wes missed and hit the wall, his fist making the hole.

That was the last straw. I turned on Mark, still on the hall floor and began a tirade. I must have frightened Wes, because he tried to defend Mark somewhat and blamed himself for the hole in the wall. I had lost patience with Mark and picked him up bodily and practically pitched him down the hall to his room. Standing in the doorway, I continued my tongue lashing. I was so loud and intense that Doris ran upstairs to calm me down. I told her to take over. I was so mad that I was afraid I might lose my temper completely and hit Mark.

One good thing came from this incident: The boys' respect for me from that point on improved considerably! They had seen that I could be pushed only so far.

Psychologically, Mark would have been considered a person with an extremely low or poor self-image. His dislike of others and his many fears were symbolic of his dislike for himself and feelings of inadequacy. Lack of acceptance by those around him disturbed him deeply. His greatest fear was of death. Each time Mark was to fly home to visit his parents and family during the holidays, we had to spend considerable time and energy convincing him the airplane would not crash and he would arrive safely. Mark would seek reassurance for several days before each flight and usually right up until he boarded the plane. His parents told us they had the same problem with him before his return flights.

The first few months Mark was ostracized by the other boys because of his attitude and none wanted him as a roommate. It was difficult to get the other boys to try to understand and accept him. Many times we thought we had bitten off more than we could chew. Were we capable of rising to the challenge Mark offered us? Yet we could see the beauty and warmth that sparkled from his eyes and knew that deep within his soul he wanted to love and be loved.

After three months with us, a slow, almost imperceptible but steady change began to come over him. We attributed the change to the spiritual focus of our family. We had a deep commitment to the Edgar Cayce readings and to their wisdom. We were active with the A.R.E. Dallas Council and involved in a lot of metaphysical activity in general. I was serving as the Texas A.R.E. Regional Representative at the time and traveling the state. In those days, we were most fortunate to be able to draw from the wisdom and experience of Hugh Lynn Cayce, Herb Puryear, and Elsie Sechrist, who came to Texas often to give lectures and workshops. I thought our involvement with the foster home program was a direct result of our daily meditations and the constant use of the affirmation on Cooperation in A.R.E.'s *A Search For God, Book I*:

> Not my will but Thine , O Lord, be done in me and through me. Let me ever be a channel of blessings, today, now, to those that I contact in every way. Let my going in, my coming out, be in accord with that Thou would have me do, and as the call comes, "Here am I, send me, use me." 262-3

We never tried to force our spiritual beliefs on the boys, but we often got into some deep, philosophical discussions after dinner. The boys were always welcomed if they chose to remain with us around the dinner table to talk. Most of the boys joined in, including Mark, who asked the most questions and showed the most interest.

The subjects that interested him most were life after death, reincarnation and karma, the spiritual laws of the universe as presented in the Edgar Cayce readings, such as the law of attraction, and the application of these laws and principles in our daily lives in order to learn to cooperate and get along with ourselves and those about us. Although Mark was not a Roman Catholic, we noticed he began attending Mass each Sunday with his Catholic roommate. He began asking to say the blessing at meal times. He became much easier to live with and the boys slowly began to accept him.

Mark had two great goals in life that he talked about constantly. One was to be accepted by his peer group, and the second, which he talked about the most, was to drive a tractor. He had a deep interest in tractors, bulldozers, and heavy machinery, as his father was an architect and his work included exposure to heavy equipment.

In early February, Kevin, one of the foster boys who lived on a farm about 40 miles south of us, invited Mark and Roo, another foster child, to spend the weekend with him on the farm. We were astonished but pleased that Kevin would invite Mark. We were also concerned because of Mark's diabetic condition; however, Kevin's father was a physician and we were assured that Mark would be looked after.

When he returned the following Sunday, you would have thought he'd been to Utopia, he was so ecstatic about the good time he had enjoyed. All he could talk about was the tractor he had driven. He was extremely tired from the visit, but he let us know in no uncertain terms that it had all been worth it. Mark's two goals had been realized. He'd finally been accepted by the other boys and, he got to drive that tractor.

I was awakened the next morning earlier than usual by Margie, Doris' mother. The look on her face betrayed her concern as she said in a broken voice, "Something is wrong with Mark."

I had a sinking feeling in the pit of my stomach, and sensed what had happened. I rushed upstairs and found Mark lying on his back in bed with his left arm dangling off the side of the bed. We rushed him to the hospital to no avail. I knew he was dead as his body was cold and he had no pulse. Mark had passed on some three or four hours previously during the night.

It was extremely difficult to call Mark's parents, the only parents we had not met in person. We had talked with them often by phone, however. If it was hard for us, it was indescribably hard for them. They flew to Dallas immediately and were the most charming and gracious couple we could ever hope to meet. They did not hold us responsible for Mark's death and were most understanding. We had checked Mark's sugar level and given him the required insulin shot just before he had gone to bed. Mark's father was also a diabetic and knew there is a possibility of an early death. We later learned it is not unusual for teenage diabetics to die from heart attacks. It was surprising yet most rewarding when Mark's parents told us we were the only individuals Mark had not criticized during his almost two years in Dallas.

We had wondered what this experience meant, but the greatest revelation was yet to come. We had felt God's hand in Mark's coming to live with us all along and knew His guidance had a purpose. We learned much through Mark's presence in our home. If each life is a preparation for the soul's next experience, we could find the meaning of these events in a remark Mark made his last night with us. He and Margie were sitting in the kitchen where Mark was having his nightly bedtime snack. Mark stopped eating a moment, looked up at Margie thoughtfully and said very matter-of-factly, "You know, Margie, I'm not afraid to die anymore."

Here, in my opinion, is a perfect example of meditation Energy in action. Mark's Higher Self, his Superconsciousness or God Self, if you wish, knew what was required to help him lose his fear of death in order for him to be able to make a peaceful transition. His soul and our souls, as his foster parents, knew that by guiding him to us for spiritual instruction, his conscious mind could lose its fear of death and be released for the transition time his own soul had selected. The Cayce readings, along with other metaphysical writings, clearly indicate we, as souls in the spiritual realm, choose our birth time and our death time prior to entering the earth in a physical body. We plan our life-to-be in the earth, including those things we want to accomplish, such as working out our karmic patterns. When we have finished our work, we leave the body by what we term physical death. This is a subject best discussed in a future book on reincarnation, for it requires much more information than space permits here.

The point is: Even though Doris and I were consciously unaware of why Mark came to us, our Higher Selves knew the score, so to speak. We were selected to serve Mark in his need. As daily meditators, we were in close contact with the God-Self within us. We had been asking to be used in serving others through the prayer/affirmation mentioned earlier, and that is exactly what happened. It is not necessary to always know how and why we are being used. If we meditate every day and we have Love, the Christ, or God as our ideal, then I can assure you we will be used, with or without our conscious knowledge. This is why I said earlier that, as our souls grow through meditation and contacting the Spirit within, we are given more and more responsibilities and opportunities to serve others.

Not all, or perhaps I should say very few, manifestations of Energy from meditation will be as dramatic as the story about Mark and his death. Most will be subtle and not even recognized by the meditator. For example, I have lectured for the A.R.E. and other organizations for more than thirty years. As all healing comes from the God within us, in a like manner, all messages and education for the searching, seeking student come from within the lecturer and the listener. For this reason, I always meditate before a lecture or a seminar. I know I am just a channel or instrument through which God speaks (as are we all). I meditate to be in touch with His wisdom and

SEEKING INFORMATION ON

holistic health, spirituality, dreams, intuition or ancient civilizations?

Call 1-800-723-1112, visit our Web site, or mail in this postage-paid card for a FREE catalog of books and membership information.

Name: _____

Address: _____

City: _____

State/Province: _____

Postal/Zip Code: _____ Country: _____

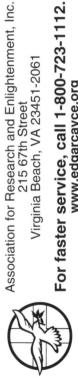

Association for Research and Enlightenment, Inc.
215 67th Street
Virginia Beach, VA 23451-2061

For faster service, call 1-800-723-1112.
www.edgarcayce.org

PBIN

BUSINESS REPLY MAIL

FIRST CLASS   PERMIT NO. 2456   VIRGINIA BEACH, VA

POSTAGE WILL BE PAID BY ADDRESSEE

ASSOCIATION FOR RESEARCH
AND ENLIGHTENMENT INC
215 67TH STREET
VIRGINIA BEACH VA 23451-9819

NO POSTAGE
NECESSARY
IF MAILED
IN THE
UNITED STATES

say those things the audience needs to hear. I have never given two identical lectures on the same subject, because each audience is different and has different needs. More than once, I have had people come up to me after a lecture and tell me of things I said twenty years ago at a lecture they attended and how much it helped them. Well, I certainly was not aware of any specific message to any particular person. I just made myself available as a speaker and let God do the work. I am reminded of the Cayce reading for a man who was told he had unknowingly saved a man's life that very morning because the reading recipient had smiled at the man. The man in question had been on his way to commit suicide, but because of the smile from a stranger, he was given a new lease on life and changed his mind about killing himself. The point the reading was trying to make was that God uses us so very, very often without our conscious knowledge. We just need to make ourselves available to His Energy and guidance through meditation. He will do the rest. It is probably best we are not aware of such frequent uses, or we might become egotistical about it and think it is we who deserve the credit.

Working with the Light also means using the Light to change oneself into a better person. We can use it to rid ourselves of negative habits and to enhance or create new positive habits and characteristics. I have personally used meditation Energy to help myself overcome a number of problems, which are, of course, simply opportunities to grow spiritually. Again, here is my personal definition of meditation: meditation is a process of letting go of the problem or situation needing a solution and turning it over to the creative Energy within. The problem with a lot of Americans is that we expect or want instant solutions. The God within us knows best the steps required to solve any problem we may have. He lives within us and knows our body, mind, and emotions far better than we. We need to be patient; some solutions require an element of time. Here's how meditation Energy helped me to quit a twenty-six-year cigarette-smoking habit:

I started smoking when I was sixteen years old. I was lucky that I never smoked more than a pack and a quarter a day. That's too much, of course, but at least I was not a three-, four-, or five-pack smoker. I started playing saxophone and clarinet in dance bands in the middle 1940s, during World War II, and musicians were in demand, as most of the eighteen- to thirty-year-olds were in some branch of the armed services. This later led me into dance band work after the war (after a stint in the Navy) as a professional musician. In those days, many people smoked, and nearly every one in the music business smoked, so my habit became ingrained quite deeply.

I had tried quitting a few times in those twenty-six years, but never quit for more than a month or two. Finally, when I was thirty-five years old, I began to really get a push to quit the habit. I had discovered the A.R.E. and the Edgar Cayce readings by then and had become a meditator. Cayce's readings emphasized good health through nutrition, exercise, and proper attention to the spiritual life. He strongly recommended daily meditation as food for the soul.

For six long years, from the age of thirty-six through the age of forty-one, I worked at trying to stop the smoking habit. I tried every device, pill, approach, technique, and plan available, but with limited success. I was able to stop smoking a number of times during this six-year period, sustaining nonsmoking spans lasting from one to three months. However, each time, I returned to the habit. I was becoming frustrated and angry. I had no control over the addiction. The tail was wagging the dog, and I did not like it one bit.

During one of my daily meditations, the thought occurred that I had not tried the one approach which I had been shown time and again produced consistent success. I had never sat down in meditation and asked the God within to take my problem on and help me to become a nonsmoker. So, on October 15, 1968, I began my evening meditation with the prayer request. The date is significant, and it is interesting that I made a mental note of the date of this effort, although not consciously. I simply told God I was fed up with the tail wagging the dog and that I really wanted to quit smoking. I let Him know I was sincere and also obviously very helpless in being able to achieve my goal. Therefore, I was asking His power, love, and intelligence to aid me in this endeavor since I was not able to do it on my own. (Three points are important here, I believe: I was sincere—I really wanted to quit the habit. Second, I gave the problem to Him. Third, I let go of it, knowing He would take care of it. I was truly letting go of the problem and trusting the power within to accomplish the task for me.) Following this meditation, I felt very relieved and comfortable. I literally forgot the problem of smoking and went about my daily business, smoking as usual.

A very interesting and fascinating scenario began to develop after a few weeks, although it required three or four months before I was aware of it. In four or five weeks, I realized I was smoking only about eighteen cigarettes a day. For about a week or ten days, I always had one or two cigarettes left in the pack. After the ten-day period, I returned to my normal pack-a-day-plus habit. Another four to five weeks down the road, I noticed I was smoking only fifteen cigarettes a day. This reduced amount, too, lasted eight or ten days. I then returned to my normal smoking level. Three to four months into this effort, I became aware of the fact that I was smoking only twelve cigarettes a day—again, for another short period of time, and then back to the pack a day.

By this time, the pattern was getting my attention. With each "cycle," the number of cigarettes dropped (without my consciously thinking about it or trying to do so), and the total number of cigarettes was always smaller than the time before. The reduced period always lasted a week or ten days, and then I always returned to my normal smoking habit. It was intriguing to me that I always went back to the normal daily habit of twenty to twenty-five cigarettes per day.

By the end of six months, I was down to ten cigarettes a day, with the usual short period of reduced smoking and a return to the full daily quota. I was dropping about two cigarettes a month on the schedule my body was being given: seventh month, down to eight cigarettes . . . eighth month, down to six . . . ninth month, down to four . . . tenth month, down to two . . . eleventh month, down to one . . . always returning to the full pack-a-day schedule after each reduction period. During the eleventh month, I had a period of no, none, zilch cigarettes per day, then returned to the full quota.

On October 15, 1969, I awakened from my nightly sleep with the feeling and the knowledge that it was finished. I had smoked my last cigarette the day before, and I knew it! This process took exactly one year from the date I turned the problem over to my Higher consciousness during my "asking for help" meditation. It still awes me to this day, the way the Spirit within gently, patiently, painlessly, and lovingly weaned me from the smoking habit. The Intelligence within knew *exactly* what my body/mind required to kick the habit. For the next six months, I had maybe two ever-so-slight desires for a cigarette, but they were so weak that I experienced no problem in ignoring them. I did gain weight for the first six months. Then, my metabolism adjusted, and I returned to my normal weight. I have been free of the smoking habit for thirty-one years now. It is an exhilarating feeling to be in control once again. I am now using the same meditation technique to overcome a lifelong sugar addiction. I see the same pattern appearing since I made my request a few months ago. We underestimate the power of the Spirit within us. Jesus gave us some clear instructions in the New Testament when he said, "Ask, and it will be given you; seek, and you will find; knock, and it will be opened to you." (Matthew 7:7) For those who feel their prayers have seldom been answered, consider what the readings say on the subject. During a reading, someone asked Cayce if God answers all prayer. He replied, "... all prayer is answered. [Just] don't tell God how to answer it." (4028-1) I would add my own statement of, "Yes, He does," with a "Yes, No, or Wait a while." Have you not often said "No" to your children when your own wisdom knew it was the best answer for the child? Have you not said to them, "Wait until you are a little older and better able to handle it"? Your own wisdom (knowledge based on your own experience) comes into play when dealing with children. Why not accept the greater wisdom of our Creator when we receive an answer of "No" or "Wait a while"?

The following is another experience of mine after asking for help during the preliminary prayer time of a meditation. The way the answer came may surprise you.

In 1980, I developed a hernia on the right side of my groin. The hernia appeared as a result of constant, deep coughing for five days during a bout of influenza. On the fifth day, I was lying in bed having a severe coughing bout, when I felt the tear occur in my groin. It did not hurt, but I knew what had happened. A small protruding pouch appeared. I checked with a surgeon; he said it did not appear to be serious and to do nothing. He said I could go the rest of my life without surgery, as apparently some do, but to return to him if it gave me any problems.

Four years later, the pouch began to get larger and to give me some minor discomfort. Again, I went to the surgeon. He again said it was my decision and that he would be glad to perform the necessary surgery, adding that the hernia appeared to be the kind that normally does not strangulate. I went home and prayed about the problem and again gave it to the God within for the correct solution. I explained to Him I had hoped to get through this life without having any bodily surgery, that I preferred to go without the surgery, but that I did not feel I was objective enough to make the right decision. The following evening, as I was watching the 10:00 p.m. news on television, I had some rather sharp pains in my lower abdomen, but not in the vicinity of the hernia. The pains lasted a few minutes. I thought it was intestinal gas and gave it no more thought. The next evening, I began having severe pains in the right side of my back in the kidney area. These pains were acute and lasted for more than an hour. I suspected the cause might be a kidney stone passing through the ureter to the bladder.

I went to see my regular medical doctor for a diagnostic check on what had happened to me. He examined my urine, found no blood, and told me to watch the situation closely over the weekend. (This visit to the doctor's office occurred on a Friday.) My son had come to spend the weekend with me, and while we were playing a game of miniature golf, I began having a repeat of Thursday night's attack, only it lasted much longer—about two hours. The attack forced me to discontinue the golf game, and my son had to drive us home.

The next day was Sunday, and I had an attack that lasted more than five hours. My son had already gone home, so I phoned my sister to come and take me to the emergency room of a nearby hospital. I walked into the ER, doubled over in pain. I was told that nothing could be done for me until I was checked in and had completed the required paper work. My sister and I sat there for forty-five minutes waiting for a doctor. At this point, I felt what I thought was a stone fall into my bladder, and the pain went away. I asked my sister to take me home, and I would see my regular doctor the next day. I had already telephoned my doctor Sunday night to apprise him of what had happened. When I got to his office, he had a urologist waiting to see me. During the urologist's examination, he saw the protruding pouch of the hernia. He looked up at me and said in a very concerned, loud voice, "How long have you had that hernia?" When I told him a little over four years, he said most forcefully, "You get that thing repaired at once!" At that point, the strong thought came into my mind that this was the answer to my prayer request.

The urologist had me follow up his examination with a procedure to determine whether any stones were present in my kidneys or urinary tract. Interestingly enough, the test showed absolutely no signs of any stones anywhere in my system. I also never passed any stones through the urethra. Of course, by then, I had already received the necessary message about whether or not to have the surgery.

I scheduled the surgery and had the hernia repaired. A significant discovery was made during the operation. Even though my hernia was not the kind that usually strangulates, the doctor said the torn tissue was beginning to wrap itself around some of my internal organs and the hernia would have strangulated in a few weeks. The condition, he said, would have been dangerous.

You may wonder why I had to go though all that pain and discomfort in order to get my answer. I can be very hardheaded, at times, about having my body cut open by a surgeon. If I had had my way, I would have delayed the surgery until faced with a strangulated condition. Sometimes, it takes a forceful message to get through to a stubborn consciousness, which I had at the time. Again, I sincerely wanted an answer to my question. I knew of my own obstinacy in such matters. I have no regrets concerning how the answer came to me. I am just grateful it came at the time it did. When we take a problem to the Light in meditation, we have to stay alert for the answer and its method of delivery. I had absolutely no doubt the urologist's recommending the surgery was the right answer to my prayer. It had a feeling of truth about it.

The stories I related in previous chapters concerning my wife's going to the hospital for a curettement and the five years of unemployment following my divorce are further evidence of being guided by the Light within. Sometimes I was aware of the guidance, and sometimes I wasn't. Often, we have to go through an experience, let some time go by, then look back on it to be able to see the lessons learned. The old cliché about hindsight having twenty/twenty vision appears to be true.

Daily meditation stimulates the inner guiding Light to become more active and fruitful, according to the needs of the meditator. It often stimulates our dream activity and helps us to better work with and interpret our dreams. In fact, the Cayce readings tell us meditation and our dreams are two of the safest and best ways to enhance soul growth and to receive spiritual guidance. I like what Dan Millman said about the Light in his book, *The Way Of The Peaceful Warrior*. In a Final Notes section he wrote, "The Light will disturb us when we're comfortable, and comfort us when we're disturbed. We turn to Spirit for help when our foundations are shaking, only to find that it is Spirit who is shaking them." I have found this statement to be so very, very true in my own life. I love the way he puts it. It could not be said better.

Meditation, over time, seems to enhance our dreams and helps us to understand them, especially those that are really important for our direction. I had *hyper* dream guidance during certain periods of my five-year cycle of unemployment. My dream activity was prolific and quite often chastising. I recall two dreams of a constructively critical nature. The first involved my being the engineer on an amusement park train for children. I was going in the wrong direction on the track, and then the train jumped the track. It doesn't require a dream expert to figure the meaning of this dream: My life was going in the wrong direction and had gotten off track. It was telling me to get back on track and go in the right direction.

The second dream was even more explicit. Depressed by my situation, I had become indolent and felt sorry for myself. I had not worked at even a part-time job in weeks. In my dream, I was at A.R.E. Headquarters in Virginia Beach, and present at Edgar Cayce's annual reading for the A.R.E. membership. I was excited to be there and to be able to observe one of his readings in person. During the reading, he suddenly stopped speaking, raised up on his couch, swung his feet off the sofa, looked straight at me, and said, "For God's sake, Harry, do something, man, do *something!*" You can be assured I got the message. Within a week, I found gainful employment.

Here is another beautiful story about using the Light. A statement in the readings reminds us: "As ye [take] the first step, the next is shown thee." (2600-2) A poignant anecdote very effectively illustrates this statement. A young boy of ten lived on a farm in the country with his parents. One very dark, blustery night, his father asked him to go to the barn, check on the animals, and be sure the door was closed securely. The boy objected and told his father he was scared to go out into the darkness to the barn, several hundred feet from the house. His father reassured him that he would be safe and asked him to fetch the lantern and come to the front porch. There, his father told him to hold the lantern up high and describe what he could see. The boy told his father that he saw the fence gate between the farmhouse yard and the barnyard. His father replied, "Fine, walk out to the gate." The boy walked to the gate. Then, his father said, "Now hold the lantern up again and tell me what you see." The son said, "I see the wagon in the middle of the barnyard." The father directed the boy to walk to the wagon, raise the lantern, and again describe what he saw. The boy said, "Oh, now I can see the barn." The boy was able to go to the barn using the light and to complete the chores. The reach of the lantern's illumination guided the youngster as he progressed to each point, accomplishing his mission. He took the first step, and the next one was shown him. In a like manner with challenges in life, we need to take the first step we can in the Light provided us. Doing this strengthens our faith and trust in God and His direction. The more we use and test our faith, the larger our faith muscles grow. Faith and patience increase by use. They slip away and atrophy when not applied.

Daily meditation gives us the Light we need to face life's problems. We realize the fulfillment of the Light by doing what the Light shows us to do in our everyday situations.

I would like to end this chapter by quoting from Neale Donald Walsch's book, *Friendship with God*. Walsch asks the following question, to which God gives His answer:

[Author:] How can I experience Ultimate Reality in any particular moment?
[God:]
Be still and know that I am God.
I mean that literally.
Be still.
That is how you will know that I am God, and that

I am always with you. That is how you will know that you are One with Me. That is how you will meet the Creator inside of you.

If you have come to know Me, to trust Me, and to embrace me—if you have taken the steps to having a friendship with God—then you will never doubt that I am with you always, and all ways.

So, as I have said before, embrace Me. Spend a few moments each day embracing your experience of Me. Do this now, when you do not have to, when life circumstances do not seem to require you to. Now, when it seems that you do not even have time to. Now, when you are not feeling alone. So that when you are "alone," you will know that you are not.

Cultivate the habit of joining Me in divine connection once each day . . . [1]

---

[1]Walsch, Neale Donald, Friendship with God: An Uncommon Dialogue. G.P. Putnam's Sons, Penguin Putnam, Inc., New York, N.Y., 1999 (p. 291).

9

Spreading the Light Worldwide

*I*n this final chapter, I will discuss the importance of
our bringing Light into the earth for the earth's own
healing and for the healing of earth's people. Mother
Earth has been named *Gaia* by our scientists, after the
Greek Goddess of the Earth. They see Her now as one
giant, self-regulating organism, of which we are an inex-
tricable part, a hypothesis that treats the planet as a living being. Metaphysically, She is a spiritual entity with a
soul. As we humans have trillions of living cells in our
bodies necessary to the function of our many parts, I
believe we serve as living cells to Mother Earth, all five

and one half billion of us. It is the macrocosm and the microcosm—as above, so below.

If you have noticed the changing weather patterns and natural catastrophes of the last two decades, you know it does not require a genius to realize that major changes and activities are occurring within the earth and Her biosphere. Many of these have been predicted by sources such as the Bible, Edgar Cayce, Nostradamus, Mary Summer Rain, the Native Americans, and many more. In fact, Edgar Cayce predicted a forty-year testing period from 1958 to 1998. It is the "time, times, and half-times" as mentioned in the Book of Daniel. Cayce reminded us that, in previous lives, many of us on earth today played a major role in the sinking of Atlantis, through our negativity and our selfishness, even though we were warned of the impending destruction in those ancient times.

We destroyed that continent by the misuse of God's energy for controlling and manipulating others. All 133,000,000 residents were either killed or escaped to other continents (Africa, Egypt, the Americas) during its sinking beneath the ocean approximately 12,500 years ago (5748-2). Atlantis developed a very high technology. Will we misuse God's energy once again? Or can we learn the Law of Love and save our planet and ourselves? The Cayce readings made a strong point by telling us that man's negative thoughts and emotions can help create storms, tornadoes, and hurricanes; that the misuse of free will causes robberies, rapes, murders, and wars (5757-1 and 195-19). Today, there are about fifty little wars in progress all over the planet. We are stripping our rain forests of oxygen-producing trees and plants. We are polluting our oceans, rivers, and atmosphere; we are detonating atomic bombs in the intestines of Mother Earth, adding stress and strain to the earth's natural fault lines. Is there no end to our selfishness and our madness?

Much dire, negative prophecy has been proclaimed for our planet, but I believe, as the Cayce readings say, that all prophecied events can be changed by our free will response to them. (1602-6) Although I see what appears to be runaway evil and repugnant negativity gaining ground on our planet, I also see an increase, however slight, in a spiritual awakening occurring among people. This gives me great hope and joy! This spiritual awakening is the result, in my opinion, of more and more people turning to prayer and meditation as a healing balm.

And here is where the significance and importance of urging people to meditate every day come into play. The Light is far more powerful than the darkness and eliminates the darkness wherever it occurs. I have alluded to the Light numerous times in this book and pointed out that we become Light transmitters when we meditate in the Silence. This Light radiates from us according to our motives, purposes, and spiritual ideals. The following is a powerful analogy, a true story, showing the power of light over the darkness.

When I was about fourteen years old, my parents took me to see Carlsbad Caverns, just south of Carlsbad, New Mexico. In 1941, the cave rangers were still taking groups through the caverns on guided tours. (Nowadays, you can walk alone through the caverns.)

When we arrived in the Big Room, which is 750 feet below the surface, the rangers did something they no longer do for present-day tourists. The Big Room has a giant-sized stalagmite named the "Rock of Ages." The tour group was seated in front of this stalagmite, and all the underground lights were turned off. I experienced the blackest black and darkest darkness ever encountered in my life. I could not see my hand in front of my face. I could not see anything! This room is about 200 feet high and about 500 feet wide. It is well over a half-mile long and curves around a bend on one end.

The rangers then did two things. The first was to have a group of them sing the hymn, "Rock of Ages," which was quite moving. It was the second event, however, that impressed me. They had one ranger stationed at the end of the room, around the bend, about 500 feet away from us. He lit a kitchen match. It was absolutely unbelievable the amount of light the match created in the darkness! We could not see the flame, of course, but the glow from it was bright enough that we could see the faces of each other in our tour group quite plainly. To say I was awestruck would be an understatement. It left an indelible impression in my memory.

Now, if one single match can create enough light to dispel the darkness that engulfed us in the cavern, just think what your spiritual Light can do to dispel the darkness found in the Earth! Darkness is the absence of light. The darkness represents how we—some of us—are using the Energy. If we don't express this Light and let it shine, are we not contributing to the darkness, whether from self-centeredness or just plain apathy? Jesus said in Matthew 5:14-16, "Ye are the light of the world. A city that is set on an hill cannot be hid. Neither do men light a candle, and put it under a bushel, but on a candlestick; and it giveth light unto all that are in the house. Let your light so shine before men, that they may see your good works, and glorify your Father which is in heaven."

We all carry this Light within us, but it is up to us to choose to use it in loving service to ourselves and to our brethren. One way we can do this is to make the choice to meditate each and every day and to ask the Christ within us to direct our lives as He would have us live it. God is a very patient God and has given us all eternity to recognize Him and to call Him forth into our lives. Even though we have eternity, the time is now, because the earth and all Her children are hungry for the Love, the Peace, and the Joy the Light can bring us.

Assuming we are also willing to express that Peace and Love, will they not spread to those whose lives we touch day by day? You've probably encountered what's come to be called the *hundredth-monkey principle*. (*The Hundredth Monkey*, by Ken Keyes, now out of print.)

Briefly, it is the story of a group of monkeys living on an island uninhabited by humans (except for the researchers studying them). One day, one of the monkeys went down to the sea shore and began washing the sand from its food before eating it. No monkey had done that before. Later, other monkeys, having observed the first one washing its food, began to wash their food also. Eventually, most of the monkeys on the island began rinsing the sand from their food prior to eating it. Still later, monkeys on another island twenty miles away also began washing their food before eating it, although there had been no physical contact with any of the monkeys on the first island. The monkeys on both islands were of the same species. The point of the story is that all of the monkeys were of the same mind-set, or, perhaps, one can say, they were all mentally connected on the subconscious level. The new idea or habit of rinsing food prior to eating it had traveled through the collective unconscious from island to island.

Cayce's readings tell us we are all connected with each other on the subconscious mind and superconscious levels. If enough of us make the God connection through meditation, can we not expect the Peace and Love we show to someday be adopted by everyone on the planet? Just think of that!

The following are a few quotes from the Edgar Cayce readings concerning the subject of meditation. Perhaps they will encourage you and stimulate you to create a daily meditation habit:

Of course, meditation . . . helps self more than self

can be aided in any other way. 3226-2

But if there is set a definite period or manner of meditation . . . there may be had a balancing. And . . . there may come an activity that will enable the body-physical . . . to "snap out" of these expressions, those depressions, those feelings of floating, those feelings of losing control, those feelings of the inability of concentration. 1089-2

. . . the quicker way [to overcome conditions of being overtired mentally and physically], the greater response, physically and mentally, may be found by the perfect relaxation in meditation . . . 257-92

As the [person] may experience in some . . . moments of meditation, the finding of peace in self enables the [person] to give more assurance, more help to others . . . 3098-2

Take time first to be holy. Don't let a day go by without meditation and prayer for some definite purpose, and not for self, but that self may be the channel of help to someone else. For in helping others is the greater way to help self. 3624-1

But whenever the body will lay aside its consciousness of material desire, and meditate upon the spiritual influences that may move upon self, better and greater will be the inflow of health, strength, resistance and constructive forces within self. 620-3

As to time—set this not as a convenience so much, but as a period when ye may commune with thyself. See thy body as the temple of the living God.

For it is there that He has promised to meet thee. 2432-1

(Q) How can I improve memory and concentration?

(A) Study well that which has been given through these sources on Meditation. Through meditation may the greater help be gained. As it has been indicated oft to the body, *do it* and leave the results to the Creative Forces; for they are a part of thee. Let thy light so shine (for thou hast gone far on the highway) that others, seeing, may take hope and find that song, too, that springs oft within thy breast. 987-2

The Christ Consciousness is defined by the Cayce readings as "the awareness within each soul, imprinted in pattern on the mind and waiting to be awakened by the will, of the soul's oneness with God". (5749-14)

When we meditate, we are doing what reading 5749-14 says. Here's another way of considering the significance and meaning of this powerful statement. We are simply becoming more and more aware of our oneness with God on a three-dimensional level, an awareness placed there by having such pattern impressed indelibly upon our mind so that, eventually, through God's patience and our searching and seeking, the knowledge and awareness will become ours consciously, and we can work with this awareness on a daily basis.

I remind you once again, we are God's highest physical expression in the earth plane, and because we have free will to accept Him or turn our backs on Him, He needs us to make the choice to become one with Him, in consciousness, in order for His Love to become fully manifest in the earth.

I leave you with this final thought and affirmation

from the A.R.E.'s *A Search For God, Book I,* from the chapter entitled "Know Thyself." It will help you to achieve two great benefits at the same time. As the affirmation takes hold in your life, it will guide and lift you to a happier, more joyful, and productive life, while, at the same time, help you to become a stronger, more useful, loving instrument and channel through which the Christ can more fully and effectively spread His Light in the earth:

Father, as we seek to see and know Thy face, may we each, as individuals, and as a group, come to know ourselves, even as we are known, that we—as lights in Thee—may give the better concept of Thy Spirit in this world. 262-5

SHALOM!

Afterword

*L*et me share with you my philosophical view on life, a metaphysical one and one that keeps me "on track" most of the time. It is derived from my studies of the Edgar Cayce readings, Rosicrucianism, Theosophy, our Christian Bible, and the Middle Eastern and Far Eastern religions/philosophies.

Our starting point should be ourselves. We have been given free will. We can no longer blame our parents, our relatives, our employers, our government, or conditions in which we find ourselves for our so-called problems. We create our own realities, although to realize it may require a broader view than looking at a single lifetime. (See the suggested reading list for books on reincarnation.)

Every situation in which we find ourselves, regardless of the cause, is an opportunity for soul growth. That's all any problem is, an opportunity for learning life's lessons. We have to be willing to change ourselves and our attitudes. The more we understand ourselves and who we are, the more we will come to love ourselves as we are loved. The more we learn to love ourselves, the more will we be able to love others—maybe not their actions, but their real selves, their spiritual selves.

Learn to enter the stillness and quietness of Spirit, from which comes our strength. Strive for balance in all things, as Paul admonished us to seek moderation in all things. Balance is an important tool mentioned throughout the Cayce readings. Dannion Brinkley often says we are all great spiritual warriors; we just need to become aware of that fact. Regardless of our greatness as souls, we should strive to let the persona stay moderate and humble. Humility does not rob us of our self-confidence. He who is willing to be last shall be first in the sight of God.

Be in the world but not of it, as Jesus instructed us. Avoid judgmental, narrow, closed thinking. Be open and receptive to others' ideas and thoughts—you might learn something! Practice living the common life we see everyday in an uncommon way. Be willing to accomplish a task for the task's sake, seeking not to receive the credit or glory for it. Should another attempt to get credit for your work, let them. It is not your problem. We reap what we sow, sometimes quickly, sometimes in a few years or maybe several lifetimes later. The universal law of karma will take care of those who abuse you or the world.

In partnerships of every kind—marital, personal, or business—consider what a partnership is. The ultimate partnership is a marriage of our higher and lower selves, our outer personality with the Christ within, blending together as one in the spirit of cooperation. Real partnerships are consummated only by individuals and whole beings who retain their separateness while functioning as one, each allowing the other to be an individual.

Be open and receptive to the gifts of the Spirit. Be alert for messages, signals, and various signs given for our direction and guidance. Many times, these messages are very subtle and difficult to grasp. Here is where daily meditation becomes a valuable tool; it helps us to gain an awareness of these signals. Guidance often comes in business meetings, chance encounters with persons much wiser than ourselves, and new connections bringing new opportunities into our lives. We can learn from everyone, even from thieves and those who practice subterfuge. Don't expect others to change. We cannot change others, but we can change ourselves as the need arises.

As a snake sheds its old skin, be willing to give up outmoded ways and self-destructive habits that may be holding back your soul growth. Sometimes, life requires us to become submissive and, perhaps, even to retreat in order to regroup and enhance our inner strengths. Don't be reluctant to give abundantly of yourself and your resources, your knowledge and experience. One cannot give with the right motive and purpose without it being returned to the giver in great abundance.

As we let go and turn to the Spirit within, new beginnings come into our lives. Positive growth and change occur, but they may involve what appears to be a descent into darkness. It is destroying the old to make way for the new. As all of nature dies in the fall and is reborn again in the spring, some, in their newfound spiritual birthing, may undergo a death within. It is simply the death of the old nature making way for the new soul expression. Spiritual rebirthing sometimes involves radical change, but such change is always accompanied by a new spiritual strength to deal with whatever changes life brings to us. Let any restrictions or restraints help us to recognize that setbacks, troubles, and problems can be our teachers and guides in developing the fruits of the Spirit, namely patience, kindness, compassion, empathy, and Love.

Souls having entered upon the spiritual path will notice they have developed an unwillingness to permit any conduct associated with their past lifestyle that creates problems or stress in their new lives. The time required to become aware of this unwillingness is relative to the soul's experience and the time the person has been on the spiritual path. It is a slow growth for most of us; some of our negative traits may be deeply imbedded. Perseverance and tenacity are needed, along with patience with ourselves, as our higher selves bring us various tests to see how well we are progressing on the path. As Spiritual Warriors, we may be called upon, from time to time, to resist the influences of the dark forces. The primary battle is with the self. Watch the emotions, both positive and negative, and work to create the daily meditation habit. Know that the activity, by its very nature, keeps us surrounded in the protective Light of the Christ. Vigilance is required by all Spiritual Warriors.

The more we seek answers, the more we ask for solutions, the more we knock on doors previously unopened to us, the more we "practice the Presence" through our meditations, the more joy will come into our lives, along with a new and heightened sense of our own wholeness and well-being. Light begins to pierce the clouds of darkness and ignorance in which we have immersed ourselves over many lifetimes. A new clarity and understanding become ours as we merge and blend the lower self with the Higher Self. From our own personal research, we become enlightened to the point that the God within can guide us into becoming stronger, more powerful instruments through which to manifest His Love in the earth.

The following Cayce reading sums up the message of this book:

Do that which is good, for there has been given in the consciousness of all the **fruits of the spirit:** Fellowship, kindness, gentleness, patience, long-suffering, love; **these be the fruits of the spirit.** Against such there is no law.

Doubt, fear, avarice, greed, selfishness, self-will; these are the fruits of the evil forces. Against such there is a law. Self-preservation, then, **should be in the fruits of the spirit,** as ye seek through any channel to know more of the path from life—from good to good—to life; from death unto life, from evil unto good. Seek and ye shall find. **Meditate on the fruits of the Spirit** in the inner secrets of the consciousness, and the cells in the body become aware of the awakening of the life in their activity through the body. In the mind, the cells of the mind become aware of the life in the spirit. The spirit of life maketh not afraid. 5752-3 [Author's emphasis in bold.]

Suggested Reading List

The Aquarian Gospel Of Jesus The Christ, Levi (Levi H. Dowling). 1972, DeVorss and Company, Marina del Rey, Calif.

At Peace in the Light, Dannion Brinkley. 1996, Harper, New York, N.Y.

Autobiography Of A Yogi, Paramahansa Yogananda. Self-Realization Fellowship, Los Angeles, Calif.

Creative Meditation, Richard Peterson. 1991, A.R.E. Press, Virginia Beach, Va.

The Edgar Cayce Primer, Herbert B. Puryear, Ph.D. 1985, Bantam Books, New York, N.Y.

Edgar Cayce's Story of Karma, Mary Ann Woodward. 1994, Berkley Publishing Group, New York, N.Y.

The Inner Power of Silence: A Universal Approach To Meditation, Mark Thurston, Ph.D. 1986, A.R.E. Press, Virginia Beach, Va.

Many Mansions, Gina Cerminara. 1999, New American Library, New York, N.Y.

Meditation and The Mind Of Man, Herbert B. Puryear, Ph.D., and Mark Thurston, Ph.D. 1999, A.R.E. Press, Virginia Beach, Va.

Paradox of Free Will, Mark Thurston, Ph.D. 1997, A.R.E. Press, Virginia Beach, Va.

The Prophet, Kahlil Gibran. 1999, Random House, New York, N.Y.

Reincarnation: An East-West Anthology, Joseph Head and S.L. Cranston. Causeway Books, New York, N.Y.

Saved by the Light, Dannion Brinkley. 1995, Harper, New York, N.Y.

The Sleeping Prophet, Jess Stearn. 1997, A.R.E. Press, Virginia Beach, Va.

A Seer Out Of Season, Harmon Hartzell Bro, Ph.D. 1996, St. Martins, New York, N.Y.

There Is A River, Thomas Sugrue. 1997, A.R.E. Press, Virginia Beach, Va.

The Way Of The Peaceful Warrior, Dan Millman. 1985, H.D. Kramer, Inc., Tiburon, Calif.

The World Within, Gina Cerminara. 1967, A.R.E. Press, Virginia Beach, Va.

Conversations with God: An Uncommon Dialogue, Books 1, 2 and 3, Neale Donald Walsch. 1995, 1997, 1998, Hampton Roads Publishing Co., Inc., Charlottesville, Va.

Friendship with God: An Uncommon Dialogue, Neale Donald Walsch. 1999, G.P. Putnam's Sons, New York, N.Y.